Friends and Neighbors

by

James L. Fleming, Jr.

Williams & Simpson, Publishers
Greenville, North Carolina

ISBN: 0-932705-07-3

*For my wife, Ellen
and for my mother.*

Robert Lee Humber

Chapter I

In writing this book I make no claim to fame or fortune other than the good fortune of having been a neighbor and a close friend of Robert Lee Humber. I relate my memories, however insignificant, in the hope that the reader will glean at least a glimpse of Robert Lee Humber's character, wisdom, and, especially, his vision, which the world so badly needs today.

In the story to follow, so little is said about the close ties of friendship between Robert Lee Humber and members of my family that I am obliged to offer a few remarks as background information. Robert's mother and father were devout Christians, whose lives greatly centered around family and church activities. Each, however, remained loyal to his or her denominational church. Mr. Humber was a member of the Jarvis Memorial Methodist Church on Washington Street, just a short distance from his home at the corner of Fifth and Washington streets, in Greenville, North Carolina. Lena Dye Humber, his daughter, attended church with her father. The other children, John, Robert, and Leslie Humber, went to church with their mother. When Robert Lee Humber, their second son, born May 30, 1898, was old enough to attend Sunday School, his mother took him two blocks from home to her church, the Memorial Baptist Church, at the corner of Fourth and Greene streets.

One of the first persons to greet Robert upon his arrival at the Memorial Baptist Church was my mother. She had been serving as volunteer organist in the Sunday School and later in the church since she was fourteen years old. The Sunday School presented her an attractive silver jewelry box engraved with the words: "To our organist Loula White from the Baptist Sunday School, Greenville, North Carolina, 1893." She was fifteen years old at that time. On June 21, 1899, she was married in that church to James L. Fleming, a local attorney, whose career of service to his community and to his state as a two-term North Carolina state senator was tragically terminated by an automobile accident only ten years and a few months after their wedding. My mother was a vivacious, petite Southern lady. Robert was an alert, thoughtful, and friendly boy. They got along fine together from the start.

Robert noticed that my mother, who was only five feet three inches tall, had difficulty reaching the pedals of the old Sunday School organ, and he told his father. Mr. Humber, a machinist by profession, went to the church, examined the organ, saw what he could do, and set about doing it. I do not recall that particular organ, which I assume was disposed of before my Sunday School days. The story I recall, however, is that Mr. Humber attached a wheel to the back of the organ, made the necessary connections to the bellows, then attached a handle to the wheel so that Robert could turn it to supply the necessary air pressure while Mother played the organ. In any case, Mother and Robert became great friends and Mother's home next door to the church, at the corner of Third and Greene streets, became Robert's second home.

In a few years my sister Louise, whom Mother had schooled to be "the perfect little lady," became Robert's childhood sweetheart. When they were teenagers, Robert made a habit of stopping by the house after church service each Sunday for a few minutes of conversation. This frequently extended to an hour or more because other church members saw the group sitting in the breeze at the southern end of the long front porch and came to join in the conversation. The only member of the family who did not like this habit was Mrs. Beulah Carney Staton, a wonderfully good woman who worked for the family more than forty years. She loved all the children, including Robert, but she was also proud of the delicious Sunday dinners she prepared and she wanted them eaten while they were hot.

Robert found in Mother not only a delightful conversationalist but an intelligent and sympathetic listener, who would respond with her honest opinion and give advice when requested. She kept up with his progress in school and later with his career. He told her his dreams and his plans, but she never repeated anything he told her in confidence. They remained loyal friends as long as they both lived. Robert's letter to her, dated January 19, 1922, gives some insight into his thinking at age twenty-three:

CENTURY CLUB
7 WEST FORTY THIRD STREET
NEW YORK

January 19, 1922

My dearest "Little Mother,"

Your letter received a most vociferous welcome. I spared only a few seconds before finding myself eagerly perusing its contents. Your letters mean much to me. I value them highly. So often I find myself wondering why the ships bring them to me so infrequently. I hope this spring—and subsequently—you will make it a positive point to see that I do hear often.

Let me first of all dispose of the project. The experience in running this down to its fundamental basis has been both intensely fascinating and extremely valuable. I regard highly the contacts established and acquaintances made. The status is this. Last spring President Aydelotte of Swarthmore College—then Professor of English in Massachusetts Tech, but both then and now American Secretary of the Rhodes Trust—submitted to the Carnegie Foundation a plan similar to mine. It had, I understand, the endorsement of the leading men of the nation.

At that time President Angell, of Yale, was President of the Carnegie Foundation. He told me that he examined the plan very carefully and gave it his approbation. In recommending it to the Board of Directors, he advised the Foundation to underwrite the appropriations for a period of from five to ten years during which time feasibility and practicality of capitalizing a Foundation particularly for this object could be ascertained. Last spring, it seems that the funds of the Foundation were abnormally low and though theoretically approving of it the Board could not see their way clear to make the necessary appropriation at that time. President Angell, however, allowed me to leave with the understanding that as soon as the Board felt financially able they would propose financing it.

Just how comprehensive President Aydelotte's scheme is I do not know. I am inclined to believe that it is merely reciprocating for the British Empire the Rhodes Scholarship idea without enlarging it, as is my plan, to include the whole world.

9

I am writing President Aydelotte—whom I knew while at Harvard—and am informing him of my proposition.

As I look back upon my past life, with the many schemes in which I have been interested—the Avon Farm, Pine Tar Oil Manufactory, Apartment House, Railroad Invention—and all—I wonder sometimes if all this experience is not, after all, just exactly what I need. Success has not crowned a single effort. Each adventure is making me more immuned to failure and disappointment. If the world, though, keeps on baffling me in my efforts, it will force me to do something grander than I have as yet dreamed of. One of these days I shall puncture this uniformly indifferent globe.

These days in New York have given me an admirable opportunity for thinking through the plans I should adopt for the future. I have tried to weigh them quietly and prayerfully too. Deep down in me there is that ineradicable feeling and consciousness that my work in life should be anchored down there. They are my people and I love them. To be a North Carolinian and a Southerner makes me very grateful indeed to the place of my nativity. I see unexampled opportunity down there to render them some service. I do not know if I can actually benefit them by going down but I believe somehow I can. I understand them so perfectly—and the field for service is so great. I believe I was born to lead those people, and if God lets me, I am willing to try.

Senator has discussed with me the feasibility of my coming to New York, suggesting the plan of my joining him in his present firm, which he thinks is a dependable probability if I desire to take advantage of it. I have thought the whole matter thoroughly through the very best I can and insofar as I am able to feel, my field of service is in the South.

Senator says since I think it hardly possible that I shall come to New York, he agrees with me in feeling that we both ought to be together. His plan is to join me in Greenville. He is one of the greatest friends a boy has ever had—any time, any where. He is a real Prince of Men. We have carefully gone over the whole situation. I have told him all. We have weighed every element involved in the best manner we could. We agree that we should practice with Mr. Harding.

Mack is definitely committed to Greenville. Tomorrow I have lunch with Folk. (He is now on the Newark Ledger.) Carey Hunter I see on my return to Europe. All are committed and working to the end of going to Greenville. If I can just get this bunch of men there and bring Horace up from Wilmington—won't it be just wonderful? Magnificent! Sublime!

I turn my eyes again towards Europe. The lustre of my going grows dim when I contemplate whom I am leaving behind. I should not hide it from you, for I feel it very deeply. I wish so much I was taking her with me. I know of what it means to me to have her with me. I know of what it would mean to us both mutually in the years ahead. To live abroad together for many months would impart to our lives an atmosphere and a spirit which would display itself throughout the passing years. Our home, itself, would be vitally changed by it and our future would possess a resourcefulness that no vicissitude of time could steal. I can see so much to be gained by ending this prolonged separation. The future has so much in store, if we can only measure up to it. To have her over there with me! Maybe—in spite of circumstance—I can. Who knows! I will if I can.

I read intently your discussion of Margaret's attitude and position toward her following the plan I submitted. I agree with you that I do not think it wise to urge her. Above all things the enthusiasm for grasping such an opportunity should be very keenly felt. Otherwise, her personality would not be receptive to all the influences which contact with that treasure house of civilizations affords. Perhaps it will be better for Margaret to go just in the summer time—when she would not have to make up the extra work. I hope she will write me all about it and how she feels.

Let me thank you for writing me about yourself. Are you quite sure that the operation is so positively simple and detached from any serious consequences? Personally I don't see how you will be able to have an operation and leave the hospital in only a few hours. Remember you promised to write me full news. I pray that your stay there will be even more successful than your hopes and expectations. Saturday on the Saxonia, I sail. Please give my love to James. My choicest love to you always. Write soon.

Your boy,

Robert

Twenty-five years later, while campaigning in behalf of the World Federation Resolution in Missouri, Robert wrote the following beautiful letter which gives some indication of the enduring quality and depth of their friendship:

May 11, 1947

My dear Little Mother,

This is your Day, and I am thinking of you as I speed across the plains of the Middle West and through some of its rugged hills.

I wish I could be there with you, talk with you and feel the impact of your vibrant personality on this, another Mother's Day. Life consists of struggles and aspirations, which a mother's heart understands and guides. She never fails to open the vista upon horizons that add significance to living and purpose to life. Your magnificent capacity for inspiration and encouragement has displayed itself with sovereign beauty from childhood and still burns like a meteor in the firmament of matured hopes and historic dreams. You will never know how much you have meant to me—and from the fullness of a grateful heart I send you on this Day my infinite appreciation and love.

This letter may not reach you before you hear the results next Tuesday at Jefferson City.

Senator Joslyn telegraphed me at Fredericksburg that the Judiciary Committee had reported the Resolution favorably by a vote of 7 to 1. The battle is now engaged. Success in President Truman's State may have rare significance for the cause!

Mother's Day greetings—and my love.

Your boy,

Robert

P.S. Please excuse delay in mailing this letter. Thought you would like to know Senate has passed the Resolution.

In 1964, as chairman of the board of deacons of the Memorial Baptist Church of Greenville, North Carolina, Robert approached Mother saying that the church had outgrown its facilities and the members were planning to build a great downtown church making use of the entire block. In fact, the board of deacons had already purchased, or obtained options, on all the property in the block except hers.

Mother and I both were proud of Robert's ability to turn a need for more space into a magnificent endeavor, embracing

12

the noblest Christian ideals, and we were also proud that the church members had accepted the plan as their will.

Mother had long nurtured the hope, however, that the house could be left as a memorial to her husband, who had worked so hard and sacrificed so much, in order to assure the passage in 1907 of his bill to establish a normal school in eastern North Carolina. Then he and Professor Ragsdale had made the house their headquarters as they drove out each day in support of the bond issues for the school. Yet it was also her church, a memorial to the State Baptist Convention, the church where she was married, the church in which she had served as volunteer organist and choir director for more than forty years, the church which all her children had joined, and it was "her boy" Robert, the chairman of the board of deacons of her church, who was asking her to sell her home to the church.

I did not know what the future had in store for us, nor how much we could count on the will of the church to carry out its plans. I did remember, however, that some years prior to that time a strong-willed member of the church was convinced that God wanted the graves of earlier members buried in the little churchyard to be removed so there would be ample space to add a new building for the Sunday School. She seemed to know God's will better than anyone else in the church, and the graves were moved to Greenwood Cemetery just off the road leading to the city dump. Maybe there would be another member of strong will and the church would carry out its plans.

In any case, I wanted Mother's decision to be her own, and I wanted her to be happy with her decision. I therefore never spoke for or against the sale of the house. Only after she had decided to let the church have it did I request that the iron-work on the property be exempt from the sale, because I as-sumed that the house would be destroyed. Robert drew up the papers giving Mother and Margaret life estate in the house.

Within a few years after the sale, the members of the church had changed their minds and wanted to leave the downtown area, whose complexion was rapidly changing. I was disap-pointed that after Mother had made a personal sacrifice for Christian reasons, the church was backing out for what ap-peared to be un-Christian reasons.

One Sunday, some months later, as I was leaving the church the new preacher stopped me and said, "I don't believe

13

that I have heard you say what you think about our decision to move to a new site to construct our new church."

I replied, "Preacher, do you want to do the Christian thing?"

"Yes."

"Do you believe in the brotherhood of man?"

"Yes."

"Then look straight down this street toward the Tar River. Do you see a group of trees on the right about three blocks down, near the river?"

"Yes."

"Well, Preacher, there used to be on that corner an attractive red brick Baptist church which was sponsored by the members of our church. It was called the Sycamore Hill Baptist Church. Now, urban renewal has destroyed that church and its members have nowhere to go. It seems to me that the Christian thing to do would be to invite those Baptist brethren of ours to come and join us in building, right here, the handsome downtown church we've been dreaming of."

I don't know whether it was the Lord or the devil telling me what to say on that occasion, but they both seemed quite pleased with my response, and the young preacher must have been absolutely satisfied, because he never asked me another question.

Following Mother's death on May 7, 1967, Robert asked me if Margaret, Louise, and I would like to make a gift to the North Carolina Museum of Art in her honor. I told him that we would, but that we wanted him to help us make an appropriate selection. Robert smiled, and I knew that he already had something definite in mind.

Mother was a gregarious person. She loved people not superficially but sincerely and, like a pretty little bird flitting from bush to bush, she went from person to person in her little social world, bringing a delightful spirit of sincerity and charm that was missed by everybody when she was not there.

Robert, whose life was dedicated to the advancement of the idea of world federation, was fond of the story of the two Greek boys who tried with their little bird to fool the oracle. Robert used that story at the end of many of his lectures on world federation, including his final speech at the Greenville Rotary Club the evening before his death. His selection of our gift to the North Carolina Museum of Art, in Mother's honor, was the well-known sixteenth century bronze statuette of *The Bird Catcher* by Giovanni da Bologna. Although it was given

14

in the names of the three of us, Robert sincerely wanted to take part in the gift with us and did so by sharing its cost.

Louise and Robert were both excellent students, and both were ambitious. They kept in touch with each other while Robert was a student at Wake Forest College. When he celebrated the end of his career at Wake Forest, as president of the senior class, he invited Louise, then a student at Meredith College, to come to Wake Forest as sponsor of his class.

Following the graduation, Robert joined the armed forces and served as a second lieutenant in the U. S. field artillery during the latter part of World War I. He was horrified by the destruction of war. His experience in the service, followed by a brief visit to the devastated areas of France and Germany, reinforced his belief that war is a horrible waste that solves no problems. His letters to Louise at that time gave an accurate account of the devastation that wars through the ages have repeatedly inflicted on the communities of northeastern France and western Germany. Here is an example:

> Chateau Thierry, France
> Monday night. 20th

> For centuries this town (Soissons) has been the center of martial combat. Starting with the defeat of Syagrius by Clovis in 486, pillaged by Charles VI in 1414, occupied by the Prussians and Russians in 1814 and by the Germans in 1870 (after a siege of 37 days) Soissons still was not freed from the ravages of war. Twice during the recent struggle it was occupied by the Germans, from September 2 to 13, 1914, and from May 29 to August 2, 1918.

Also included in these letters, incidentally, were bits of heather picked in the fields and a sprig of leaves which the custodian of Beethoven's apartment in Bonn took from a vase in Beethoven's room and gave to Robert to send to Louise. Following the war, Robert returned to America and entered Harvard University. There he tutored history, government, and economics while earning his master's degree. Also during this time his award of a Rhodes Scholarship, to begin the following year at Oxford University, was announced.

Meanwhile, Louise was accepting roles of leadership among the students of Meredith College, and her studies leading to the A. B. degree included courses that would help her to become a pioneer career woman. She became president of the student body her senior year and, after receiving her A. B. degree, went to Columbia University for her master's degree. Following graduation there, she took a position as a counselor, first at the University of Washington in Seattle, then ten years later at Northwestern University in Evanston, Illinois. Later she became a member of the National Council of the YWCA in New York City. Finally, at the request of her aging mother, she accepted a position nearer home, as dean of students at Meredith College in Raleigh, North Carolina.

On April 8, 1980, her eightieth birthday anniversary, I dropped in to see her in her Bechanna apartment in Raleigh, where she was living in retirement. I found her busy working on a report for a committee to which Governor Hunt had appointed her. I interrupted her long enough to wish her a happy birthday and to chat for a while. During our conversation I asked, "Louise, why didn't you marry Robert?" Without hesitation she replied, "Robert and I were both persons of strong will, and I was afraid we might not make a go of it."

Since Louise's death on January 20, 1984, I have read many wonderful letters from students she counseled and from her colleagues and friends. In a sense Louise was a missionary who loved to work with people, not to persuade them to believe as she did, but to help them to analyze and understand their own problems. After reading the letters she received, I am convinced that she lived a beautiful and rewarding life, and I knew Robert Lee Humber well enough to be able to say the same of him.

During my high school years, after Robert had left Greenville, I became quite close to his younger brother, Leslie, who was much nearer my age. In 1924, Leslie and I, wanting "to see the world," spent the summer working as ordinary seamen. We were both greenhorns, but we had great fun working our way from Norfolk, Virginia, to New London, Connecticut, by barge. Then we worked as ordinary seamen on an oil tanker from New York City to San Pedro, California, via the Panama Canal. When school opened in September, Leslie, an entering freshman, became my roommate at Wake Forest. He was a fine specimen, six feet tall, liked by everyone, and he was trying out for the football team.

16

One day he came in with a pain in his side and decided to go to the college infirmary. There he was put to bed, where they kept him through the next day while they tried to determine what his problem was. Fearing it might be appendicitis, they sent him to a well-known surgeon in Raleigh, who took additional time to make sure the diagnosis was correct. The operation was performed, but it was too late. The appendix had ruptured, and Leslie was lost. His loss was a painful shock to his family and to his many friends.

Three years later, when I graduated from Wake Forest, I still did not know what I wanted to do. When Robert heard that I was undecided, he suggested to my mother that she give me a few years of study in Paris. She did, and when I arrived in France, Robert treated me as a younger brother, helping me to plan my first courses. My education began anew in a beautiful new language among people who loved their language and literature and were proud of the clarity of its prose and the music and harmony of its poetry. Once I had penetrated the veil of a foreign language, I began to understand and appreciate the maturity of the people and the age of their civilization. A few years in the beautiful capital city of this new, old world enabled me to see my own country objectively for the first time in my life.

I was not the student that Robert and Louise were. I had never developed the self-discipline necessary to become a top student, and I had the wasteful habit of taking the courses that were interesting to me rather than just those which lead to a degree.

On October 16, 1929, after two years in France, I had the pleasure of serving as best man in the wedding of Robert Lee Humber and Lucie Berthier in Paris. A little more than a year later, on November 21, 1930, after I had returned to America to face the depression as a teacher of French, I received this cablegram: "Affectionate greetings to my uncle Jim on this my first day in the world. Mama's condition fine. Marcel Berthier Humber."

While teaching at Guilford College, I used the summer months to take graduate courses that appealed to me at different universities: the University of Miami at Coral Gables, Florida, the University of North Carolina, at Chapel Hill North Carolina, and Emory University in Decatur, Georgia. At Emory I attended a language institute, taking courses with Professor Goodyear, chairman of the department, and

Professor Rochedieu, visiting professor from Vanderbilt University in Nashville, Tennessee. At the end of that summer I had the pleasant surprise of being awarded the De La Boulaye Medal for proficiency in French and of being offered graduate scholarships at both Emory and Vanderbilt. But I had already decided to attend Harvard University.

After completing my master's degree at Harvard University, I returned to Paris to seek a Doctorate from the University of Paris. Robert and I were together again, but living, this time, in different worlds. Robert was a business executive and I was once again a student in Paris.

Chapter II

At a sidewalk café in the Latin Quarter of Paris just prior to the outbreak of war in 1939, a group of students was lamenting the fact that man, in all his wisdom accumulated through the ages, hasn't yet been able to create a world organization capable of maintaining world peace.

"It would be up to your country, the United States of America, the most powerful of the democracies, to lead the way," said one, looking straight at me.

"But she is not ready to accept such an awesome responsibility," said another. "She has not fought a world war on her own soil as we have. She has not suffered the humility of witnessing the destruction of her homes and the rape and murder of members of her family. America is not ready to lead the way to a lasting peace."

Some days later at the Colisée Café where Robert and I often met for an afternoon tea break, I told him of our conversation on boulevard Saint Michel.

"You know," said Robert, "it would be relatively easy for the people of the United States to accept a world government of limited powers based on a democratic federal system. It has been estimated," he continued, "that of the laws that govern us in the United States, approximately 70 percent are made within the bounds of the individual states and 30 percent are passed by the federal government. Thus, a man who gets in trouble with a local law seeks justice before a local court, a state law, a state court, and a federal law, a federal court. We could transfer to a world federal government as little as 5 of the 30 percent of laws now passed by our federal government and that should be sufficient to assure the freedom of man and, at the same time, limit the power of the world federal government to the minimum necessary to maintain world peace. Nations would then be able to enjoy their

19

languages, customs, and traditions without fear of interference, and the huge sums of money, no longer needed to feed numerous insatiable national military machines, would become available to those nations for the enrichment of the lives of their citizens."

In the years just prior to 1939, the French people found it difficult to believe that Adolph Hitler, who reminded them so much of Charlie Chaplin, was a serious warrior. They became convinced, however, after two years of Nazi programmed threats and crises which sent Sorbonne professors (including one of mine who limped because of a wound received in World War I) scurrying from their classrooms to the Maginot line and young Frenchmen to the front at the very time they were most needed on the land. The disruption of daily life and the uncertainty and fear of what tomorrow might bring led many to conclude that war itself could be no worse than continued uncertainty. "There are worse things than death, you know," said one of my friends.

As the Nazi invasion of Poland was launched, refugees from a number of European countries began to appear in the Latin Quarter of Paris. Some were penniless. Two, to my knowledge, brought only musical instruments with them; one, a violin and the other, a handsome accordion of which he was an absolute master. Paris seemed to welcome all the refugees, just as she had received the White Russians in the years immediately following the Bolshevik Revolution.

When the declaration of war was announced over PTT on September 3, 1939, the French people, weary of the war of nerves, exhaled a deep sigh of relief and immediately inhaled a chestful of pride. *La France* had kept her promise to Poland. Now both the French students and the student refugees in Paris were in a mood to celebrate.

A French student and I joined a small group of refugees who were planning to meet others at La Rotonde later that evening. We took a shortcut through the Luxembourg Gardens. As we were passing the Senate House, someone suggested that we might be wise to stop at a reasonably priced student restaurant and get a bite to eat before going to La Rotonde for our celebration. Recalling an excellent little student restaurant in the Rue de la Grande Chaumière which I had frequented some years previously, I suggested that we stop there. Along the way I described the little restaurant as I remembered it.

It was called "Chez Wadja." Monsieur Wadja, owner and chef of the restaurant, went to Les Halles early each morning to get fresh food for his customers. Madame Wadja worked wherever she was needed, but her principal job was guardian of *la caisse*, which was located on a high table between the entrance to the restaurant and the kitchen door. Then there was Alice, the only waitress in a restaurant which could seat between thirty-five and forty persons. An attractive woman in her early thirties, Alice was always in complete control of what appeared to be absolute chaos. She was quick-witted and capable of returning just about as much good-natured ribbing as she received. Tipping was optional. There was a porcelain well sitting on the high table near *la caisse*. You could drop in a tip as you left, if you wished.

Everybody loved Alice. As regular customers entered the restaurant, even before taking a seat, they started calling for her. Alice just as quickly responded, "Attends mon petit chou, ce n'est pas encore ton tour à toi."

Someone would call out, "Alice, du Chateau de la pompe a drink always on the house, s'il vous plaît." Occasionally came the response, "vas le chercher toi-même."

One day Mr. Odell, a South Carolinian who was finishing his studies for the *Doctorat de l'Université* at the time, introduced a few of his British friends to the little restaurant. They were rather formal and perhaps a little ill at ease at first. In order to break the ice and help them join in the spirit of the place, Mr. Odell turned to Alice as she started to the kitchen with their order and said, "Alice, apportez-nous cela damn quick, n'est-ce pas?" His British friends smiled. Alice did not reply, but as she passed my table, she leaned over to my ear and said, "Monsieur Fleming, que veut dire damn quick?"

"Oh, Alice," I said, "c'est terrible. Il ne faut pas dire çela. Qui vous a dit ca?"

"Monsieur Odell," she replied.

"Ecoutez, Alice," I said, "la prochaine fois qu'il vous dit cela, dites-lui, 'Go to hell.'"

The British guests became more relaxed as they enjoyed their delicious meal. Meanwhile, I ordered another cup of coffee, which I sipped very, very slowly. After a while Alice returned to Mr. Odell's table, cleared the dishes, and, oddly enough for Alice, stood silently by while Mr. Odell took the orders for dessert. As he gave Alice their order he noticed how quiet she was and repeated, "Et Alice, n'oubliez pas. Apportez-nuis cela damn quick, n'est-ce pas?" Alice, who really didn't know how to be angry with anyone, stopped, stood erect, and looking down her nose at Mr. Odell. She said in the sweet voice of an angel but with a delightfully devilish French accent, "Monsieur Odell, go to hell."

As we approached the little restaurant, the first thing we saw was a large sign on the door: FERMÉ. Another casualty of the times, we thought, as we continued a short distance to La Rotonde at the intersection of the Boulevard Raspail and the Avenue du Mont Parnasse.

When we told the head waiter at La Rotonde that others were coming and would bring a violin and an accordion with them, he knew what to expect. He led us through the main section of the restaurant, where the paintings of contemporary artists lined the walls, to doors which opened into a large room near the rear of the restaurant. There, in that room, we enjoyed a glorious evening of music, singing, in French and English, songs of every type imaginable, from children's and students' songs to Viennese waltzes and opera. Then we listened in rapt silence to the beautiful gypsy music of the violin softly accompanied by the accordion.

At midnight, as we prepared to leave, we noticed that the doors to the back room had been opened and the restaurant was filled with people who had drifted in to listen to the music. As we came out of the back room, we were greeted by a burst of applause as many left their tables and came to shake our hands and embrace us. It was only then that we saw the tearful eyes of men and women in whom the music had awakened fond memories and, who, perhaps more clearly than we, sensed the paradoxical picture of carefree youth cast so sharply against the horror and sorrow of a war that was just beginning.

Parisians who owned vacation houses at the beach or who had kinsmen living in the provinces to the southwest sent their families away from the city. There was no longer any reason for students whose professors were now in uniform to remain in Paris. Many left with their families, and a number of foreign students returned to their homelands. Yet many of us, still clinging to the hope of being able to complete our studies, remained in Paris.

I was living at that time in a small room under the roof of

the church house, adjoining the sanctuary of the American Church in Paris. Over the years the congregation of this first American church to be established on foreign soil (1857) had moved whenever their facilities became inadequate. Their last move was from a small church on the Rue de Berry, a block or so off the Champs-Elysées. From there they moved across the Seine to the corner of Quai d'Orsay and Rue Jean Nicot (nicotine) on the Left Bank, where a tobacco warehouse once stood.

They built on that site, facing the Quai d'Orsay and the Seine River, a handsome, contemporary, Gothic edifice with ample space to accommodate the numerous and varied programs of an active congregation. It was an interdenominational Protestant church, but its Students' Atelier, which was open to all American students in Paris, included Roman Catholics, Orthodox Catholics, Jews and an occasional Moslem. We were certainly not uniform, but we were united in spirit. Occasionally an eyebrow would rise when someone expressed some unusual religious belief, but there was never any attempt at ridicule. I suppose we assumed that, in the final analysis, religion is basically a personal and private relationship between man, his conscience, and his God. I remember thinking one day that if Voltaire could look in on us, he would probably say of us, as he did of the Quakers in England, that we "astounded all Christendom by behaving like Christians."

The large Gothic edifice offered excellent facilities for student activities. In the basement, there was a gymnasium including a basketball court and two bowling alley lanes. The ground floor of the church house featured a well-equipped theatre. The second floor housed a kitchen and a large dining room, which doubled as a lecture room or a concert hall. The most popular room on this floor, however, was a handsomely furnished reading room and lounge with a large open fireplace. It was in this room that most of our informal discussions took place. The third floor housed the living quarters of the minister and his family.

Rev. Clayton E. Williams, who became minister of this American Church in Paris at the close of World War I, was still serving the church in 1939. On that September weekend when war was declared, Mr. Williams was on vacation in America. In fact, following the suggestion of our mutual friend, Robert Lee Humber, he was filling the pulpit of our home church, the Memorial Baptist Church on Greene Street in Greenville, North Carolina, that Sunday and was a guest in my mother's home next door to the church. Upon learning of the declaration of war, Mr. Williams, of course, was anxious to return to his family. My sister Margaret and her husband, Dr. John L. Winstead, Sr., who had driven him to visit Duke University, the University of North Carolina, and Wake Forest University the day before, took him the next day, September 4, to Rocky Mount, where he boarded the Atlantic Coast Line train for New York.

Meanwhile, at the American Church in Paris, scheduled programs continued as usual. One of our student programs at that time was a lecture by Alexander Kerenski, head of the provisional government of Russia until it was overthrown by the Bolsheviks in 1917. Although his English was not perfect, he was very interesting, and he seemed to enjoy our tough questions in the discussion period following his lecture. Since he was planning a lecture tour of American colleges and universities in the spring, he expressed the desire to return and speak to us again before going to America. We scheduled him for a second lecture early in the spring of 1940.

Another of our student programs at the time was a piano and violin concert by Nadia Tagrine and her brother. Nadia was an attractive person and an excellent pianist. She and her brother, a violinist, had played as a team since childhood and had given concerts in a number of the capitals of Europe. Their parents were White Russians who fled to Paris at the time of the Bolshevik Revolution. Nadia and her brother, however, were reared in Paris and were loyal to France. In 1944, while fighting in the battle for the liberation of Paris, her brother was shot from a rooftop and a distraught Nadia went into mourning. Since that time she has had only her music to live or and that, of course, is always a bitter reminder of her great loss.

The war was disrupting the .. s of young and old alike. Mr. and Mrs. Frank M. Armington, who came to the American Church in Paris as students at the turn of the century, were now having to uproot themselves from the beautiful city of Paris, which had become home, and from the church they had served so long. Mr. Armington was the artist who painted the beautiful triptych which stands in the chancel of the church and whose etching of the church is still printed on church stationery. His letter announcing their departure appeared in the church bulletin:

To the Prudential Committee
The American Church in Paris

In a few days Mrs. Armington and I are leaving for America where we will probably make our home. We had hoped to live on in Paris for the rest of our days, but circumstances of health have obliged us to make this change in our plans, which we regret very much.

We will always miss the American Church in Paris, where we have tried to do our part.

We love this church and have enjoyed our work here. We will miss our friends.

As our real home is in the life beyond, the separations here are but for a little while.

Before we leave, our hearts turn to think of the future of this Church in its work.

There is not much we can do, but, to lighten the burden and, that we may still have some part in this work, Mrs. Armington and I have arranged with the Chairman of this committee, Mr. Humber, that certain investments amounting to ten thousand ($10,000) dollars, in addition to what we have already given, be turned over to this committee with the understanding that we receive the profits during our lifetime.

We pray for the work of this Church and for those who will carry on, every blessing.

Frank M. Armington

The night of our first air-raid alarm, I was at Villeneuve St. Georges at the home of Madame Berthier, where I had lived when I first visited France in 1927. Robert Lee Humber, now Mme. Berthier's son-in-law, had just returned from Hendaye Plage in the southwest corner of France, where he had left Mme. Berthier, his wife Lucie, and their children in a safe haven near the Spanish border.

Madame Berthier's home at Villeneuve St. Georges is near the top of the hill overlooking the valley of the Seine, which leads into Paris some distance away. Many times in the past, I had stood on the balcony of that third-floor room and gazed at the lights in the valley below, which seemed to reflect the Milky Way above. This night, too, the sky was clear and the stars were shining brightly, but the lights in the valley were not responding to the beauty of the heavens above, and the Eiffel Tower, which used to appear like a brightly lighted toy on the horizon, dared not reveal its location. Frustrated young Nazis, indoctrinated since childhood to believe their racial superiority, were stalking the land with murder weapons in hand, anxiously seeking to prove their superiority. The earth was shrouded in darkness.

When the air raid alarm sounded, I put on my robe and slippers and went downstairs. Robert joined me at the second floor, and we descended into the garden where we walked and talked and watched the sky. After a while a small French plane passed overhead with its lights brightly blinking. It turned westward toward the airfield at Orly and disappeared. We finally decided to go in the house and turn on the radio. As the sound came on, a speaker was saying, "London, will you call Paris." London called Paris but there was no response. Then the speaker, Mr. H. V. Kaltenborn, excitedly pronounced, "Ladies and gentlemen, this signifies to me that Paris is now suffering her first air raid of the war." He almost frightened me.

The changes that were rapidly taking place in France are probably best depicted in the following excerpts taken from Rev. Williams' letter to my mother, telling her of his return to Paris and giving a glimpse of the church and student activities at that time:

> After fourteen days on the ship, I arrived in France, one of the fortunate few who secured permission to leave the United States and to enter France.
>
> Of course I found France changed. To begin with there was the endless but necessary red tape, inevitable at such a time for precaution and safeguard, but we found it very hampering for a few days. In consequence we had photographs taken of all the family and each of us by the dozens, and filled out endless blanks and questionnaires to get permits to travel from one province to another, to drive a car, to get gasoline and to assure our identity and safe conduct. Now most of these things are forgotten or ignored because they have become routine.
>
> The Declaration of War had meant that many of the American organizations had closed—our clubrooms were more in use than ever, and the lack of heat in many apartments made our fireplace greatly appreciated.
>
> The streets are so dark and the means of transportation

so limited that we move everything up an hour or so, but even with that, many of the young people stay on after the subways have closed and walk home.

Tea is served in the student club-room three afternoons a week and a most friendly atmosphere reigns there. One of the friends of the church, Mr. Steinhardt, has given us some additional leather furniture and provided curtains so that we can have lights on at night. The curtains are very attractive and add much to the charm of the room. The bowling alleys are being used constantly and our basketball group is using the gymnasium.

On Sunday the twenty-fourth we began our Christmastide activities with the morning service and Christmas sermon in the main church, and a Candlelight service at four o'clock, just at dusk to avoid having the Church windows too brilliantly and too dangerously lighted. The Church was lighted with a cluster of four candles at the end of each pew and rows of candles in the chancel with two large candlesticks on each side of the silver cross on the Communion table altar, and a large red two-inch Yule candle in the center of the chancel. It was a very beautiful service and very well attended.

After that we had our regular student supper with about sixty at the table, and then again this year the students went out and search-ed the river banks, under the bridges, in the subways and at the central market for "clochards" (tramps and beggars) and brought in twenty-nine of them from the cold, serving them a hot dinner in the beautifully decorated hall on the second floor. They were about equally divided, men and women, and in rags and tatters. After a delicious meal with everything except the proverbial wine and champagne, they stayed on and talked about the tables for an hour or so, after which they were given subway money and sent on their way. One old blind Viennese Jew who has been a refugee in France for the past six years, arrived at the Church without an overcoat and with his trousers slashed from the knee to the cuff. He was too old to go out into the cold again and was made comfortable for the night next to a warm radiator and sent off the next morning with breakfast and an overcoat. It took about two hours to find these beggars since there are comparatively few in Paris, and most of them are taken care of by the City or State. They were all very grateful and very happy when they left. The students paid for the dinner, presenting me the money in a gift pocket book and a poem.

In January of 1940 several members of the Students'

27

Atelier who had decided to join the American Volunteers' Ambulance Corps asked Mr. Williams if he would hold a service in the American Church in Paris to dedicate the John J. Pershing section of the American Volunteers' Ambulance Corps with the French army. Mr. Williams was delighted that they had asked him, and he immediately invited other religious leaders in Paris to take part in the service with him. The service was held February 4, 1940, with the Cathedral Church of the Holy Trinity and the American Church in Paris participating. It was such a beautiful service, and I was so impressed with Mr. Williams' charge to the men that I asked if I might have a copy. He had only the original and one copy.

The charge pronounced by Rev. Clayton E. Williams at the American Volunteers' Ambulance Corps Dedicatory Service held in the American Church in Paris—February 4, 1940:

> The cause to which you have dedicated yourselves by enlistment in The American Volunteers' Ambulance is one of the highest known to humanity, that of the giving of oneself to the succor of human life.
>
> During these past few months many have found that Destiny has rudely laid upon them the obligation to take life; yours is the privilege to save it; others must destroy, you will preserve! That is a High and Sacred Calling and one that will demand the best that is in you of Courage and Fortitude, of Perseverance and Patience, and above all, of Fidelity to Duty.
>
> The days will try you! When the first flush of enthusiasm has waned and the spirit of adventure has lost its allure, the real time of testing will come, when there will be nothing left to keep you going except your unswerving loyalty to duty and response to need. Happy will be the man who is sustained then by a Deep Faith in the Ideal which he serves.
>
> And now, as you go forth to active duty, we, who have confidence in you and in the cause to which you are dedicated, would lay this charge upon you:
>
> 1. That You be loyal, diligent and uncalculating in the pursuit of your service in the spirit of Him who came not to be ministered unto but to minister, counting no sacrifice too great where the saving of life is concerned,
>
> 2. That Your Service be impartial, extended to all men alike, regardless of race or creed, color or nationality, without distinction of rank or birth,

3.   That Your Personal Conduct be above reproach, that you be brave and true, charitable in your judgments, patient in difficulty, disciplined in spirit; and in all things worthy of your friends, your Country, and your God.

In closing I can think of no words more appropriate to the occasion than those of our Martyred President, the Great Emancipator, Abraham Lincoln—that "With malice toward none, with charity for all, with firmness in the Right, as God gives you to see the right, you may finish the work you are in, binding up nations' wounds, caring for him who shall have borne the battle"—both friend and foe in loyal service until that day when shall be achieved a lasting and righteous peace.

May God bless you!

There were twenty-five volunteers in this group. The Myron T. Herrick section of twenty volunteers was formed later, and a similar dedicatory service was held for them on April 14, 1940, in the American Church in Paris at 65 Quai d'Orsay.

A
SERVICE
TO DEDICATE

THE JOHN J. PERSHING SECTION
OF
THE AMERICAN VOLUNTEERS' AMBULANCE

WITH THE FRENCH ARMY 1939
A UNION SERVICE HELD IN

THE AMERICAN CHURCH IN PARIS

65, QUAI D'ORSAY, VIIe
SUNDAY FEBRUARY THE FOURTH
NINETEEN HUNDRED AND FORTY

THE CATHEDRAL CHURCH OF THE HOLY TRINITY
AND
THE AMERICAN CHURCH IN PARIS
PARTICIPATING

A SERVICE TO DEDICATE
Ten o'clock

Organ Prelude: "Piece Heroique" .... Cesar Franck

Processional Hymn 283: "Let There be Light:."

Sentences and Lord's Prayer and Response:
> The Very Rev. Frederick W. Beekman D. D.
> Dean of the American Cathedral Church of the Holy Trinity.

Scripture Lesson: Luke 10: 25-37
> The Rev. Clayton E. Williams,
> Pastor of The American Church in Paris.

Anthem: "Come Ye Blessed" .... Edmund Pendleton
> (Composed specially for this occasion.)

> "Come ye blessed of my Father, inherit the kingdom
> prepared for you from the foundation of the world.
> For I was hungry,
> And ye gave me meat;
> I was thirsty
> And ye gave me drink;
> I was a stranger
> And ye took me in,
> Naked
> And ye clothed me,
> I was sick
> And ye visited me
> In prison
> And ye came unto me.
> "Verily I say unto you, inasmuch as ye have done it
> unto one of the least of these my brethren, ye have
> one it unto me."
> "Come ye blessed of my Father."
>
> (Matthew 25:34)

Prayers .... The Very Rev. Frederick W. Beekman D. D.

Charge to the Members of the John J. Pershing Section.
> The Rev. Clayton E. Williams

The Offering .... For the benefit of the staff
> of the John J. Pershing Section

Offertory. Organ Improvisation.

Recessional Hymn 50: "Lead On, O King Eternal."
>(During which the Color Bearers, the Guests of Honor and the
Congregation will leave the sanctuary in the order named,
the concluding part of the service being held out-doors in front
of the Church.)

The Act of Dedication (In front of the Church.)........ The Very Rev. Frederick
W. Beekman D. D.

Benediction... The Rev. Clayton E. Williams

Following the service this morning the ambulances will proceed to the Unknown Soldier's Tomb to lay a wreath there.

The regular morning services of the American Church and the American Cathedral Church of the Holy Trinity will be held as usual at ten forty-five o'clock, in their respective churches.

MEMBERS OF THE JOHN J. PERSHING SECTION

L. A. Jump	Ambulance No	1
Phillips Muhr	>	> 2
David F. Edgar	>	> 3
Ignatius McLaughlin	>	> 4
Arthur Stratton	>	> 5
Alex. Moore, Jr.	>	> 6
Frank F. O'Neill	>	> 7
Jack Calhoun	>	> 8
Paul Brooks Willis	>	> 9
Charles Philip Braxton	>	>10
Jack Billey	>	>10
Lloyd Moore	>	>11
Charles Willen	>	>11
F. G. Fontanals	>	>12
Charles C. Ahrenfeldt	>	>13
Raoul Jacques Hammond	>	>14
Joseph Maronna	>	>14
Thomas G. Esten	>	>15
Kenneth C. Banfield, Jr.	>	>16
Richard Slomon	>	>17
Robert Monroig	>	>18
Albert Hochsteter	>	>19
Henry Peter Daymont	>	>19
Charles Francis Sweeny	>	>20
Robert M. Hiatt	>	>20

Chapter III

The nearer we approached springlike weather, the greater the probability of a Nazi offensive and the smaller our group became. Programs involving large numbers were no longer scheduled. Our informal discussion group, however, continued to meet in the library lounge, where we sat around the large open fire. We usually began our discussion by examining the latest newspaper map of the front, often trying to estimate how much farther the Nazis had advanced than the newspaper reports revealed. Then we exchanged news items and rumors we had heard during the day. The first news item I reported came by letter from a French friend who had been sent to the front near Sedan, at the western end of the Maginot line. The French government had never been willing to extend the Maginot line between France and her ally Belgium. Such would have been tantamount to saying to her ally: we will fight on your soil. In his letter my friend complained significantly that all he had done since he was called up was dig trenches. It was in this area that the Nazis later began their spring offensive.

Another bit of information I reported seemed to indicate that the Nazis had already tested the advance defenses of the Maginot line. At a sidewalk café I talked with a former student who was on a week's leave from the front. According to his story, he had been on duty in a pillbox in front of the Maginot line in the Saar area when he spotted Nazi soldiers infiltrating the valley below. He reported it and awaited orders. No signal to open fire was given until many troops had passed into the valley. Some were nearing the main line of fortification, and others were turning toward his outpost. When the order finally came, all he had to do was throw a switch and witness the slaughter. The machine guns in the area were calculated to cover almost every foot of ground in the valley. Within a few minutes the valley was covered with the dead and dying. The fear and horror of untimely death quickly ended for the young Nazi soldiers in the valley, but the young Frenchman had merely passed the first test of a soldier. He had obeyed the rules of war. He had seen and reported the infiltration. He had set up and triggered the carnage. He had witnessed the fright and pain of death on the faces of his nation's enemies. In that skirmish he was the victor, if there is a victor in war, and he would carry the memory of his victory the rest of his life or at least until he was mentally dead. It was obvious in talking with him that he needed far more than his week in Paris.

After we had covered the current war news, we usually turned to discussion of the peace that would follow the war. Many theories were advanced. We discussed each as objectively as possible, drew whatever conclusions we could, and went on to the next one. In his letter of March 13, 1940, to my mother, Rev. Williams wrote: "Little by little our group is diminishing, though the interest in the discussion of *Union Now* by Clarence Streit continues. It is James's favorite topic of discussion as he is its chief propagandist." We were intrigued for a while with the ideas expressed in Clarence Streit's *Union Now*. In fact, only a few months after we discussed his book, Winston Churchill proposed to French Premier Reynaud a declaration of permanent union of France and Britain. Meanwhile, however, our discussions were leading us to face the necessity of a broader, all-inclusive world order. We began to discuss world federation, which, at least in theory, seemed to possess the unique quality of being able to maintain peace among the nations of the world without radically upsetting the traditional way of life within their national boundaries.

I was happy to see the group move toward the discussion of world federation because I was thoroughly familiar with the theory and had confidence in its potential. It was thanks to Robert Lee Humber that I was introduced to the subject soon after I arrived in France on my first visit in 1927. At that time Robert proposed a weekend bicycle trip in order to familiarize me with the French countryside. He rode his British-made Humber bicycle with gearshift. I rode a borrowed French bicycle with no gearshift. By nightfall of the first day, I was exhausted, and we stopped some distance from the nearest town. On our right was a woods; on our left was a large field which was apparently being prepared for grazing. The grass was luxuriant. We lifted our bicycles over the fence, climbed over, and made our beds. Since we had not planned to camp out, we had not brought the proper equipment. I pulled some grass and made a pillow, which I rolled into place near the rear wheel of my bicycle. Then I put on my sweater and stretched out for the night. Robert made a similar bed beside his bicycle.

Lying there on my back under the stars, the first words that came to my mind were "Mica mica parva stella," a Latin verse I had been taught when I was a child. Robert asked if I still liked poetry. I told him that I did, in spite of the fact that at one time a very effeminate professor of English poetry had almost destroyed my interest. When he read to us in class, he first carefully placed his text directly in front of him, then daintily picked up a pencil almost by its point, and lightly marked the place where he wished to begin reading. Then, without raising his head, he looked over his glasses to see if we were ready for him to begin. Then he wet his lips with his tongue, pursed his lips, and with fastidious precision read from John Milton's "L'Allegro" (1632):

Come, and trip it as ye go
On the light fantastick toe,
And in thy right hand lead with thee,
The Mountain Nymph, sweet Liberty.

By that time my knee was cocked and my foot was itching to fly straight into the seat of his pants. I found it extremely difficult to concentrate on the meaning and beauty of poetry when he read it.

After a few moments of contemplating the stars in silence, I recited a little poem by Sir Oliver Herford entitled "Earth."

If this little earth to-night
* Suddenly should fall through space*
In a hissing, headlong flight,
* Shrivelling from off its face,*
As it falls into the sun,
* In an instant every trace*
Of the little crawling things—
* Ants, philosophers, and lice,*
Cattle, cockroaches , and kings,

> *Beggars, millionaires, and mice,*
> *Men and maggots,—all as one*
> *As it falls into the sun,—*
> *Who can say but at the same*
> *Instant from some planet far*
> *A child may watch us and exclaim;*
> *"See the pretty shooting star!"*

Robert expressed his preference for Alfred Tennyson and quoted from "Locksley Hall":

> *For I dipt into the future, far as human eye*
> *could see,*
> *Saw the Vision of the world, and all the wonder*
> *that would be;*
>
> *Saw the heavens filled with commerce, argosies of*
> *magic sails;*
> *Pilots of purple twilight, dropping down with*
> *costly bales;*
>
> *Heard the heavens fill with shouting, and there*
> *rained a ghastly dew*
> *From the nations' airy navies grappling in the*
> *central blue;*
>
> *Far along the world-wide whisper of the south-wind*
> *rushing warm,*
> *With the standards of the peoples plunging thro'*
> *the thunder-storm;*
>
> *Til the war-drum throbb'd no longer and the*
> *battle-flags were furl'd*
> *In the Parliament of man, the Federation of the*
> *world.*

We marveled at Tennyson's vision of 1886 and spent the next few hours discussing world federation before going to sleep.

I was glad that the subject of world federation had come up for discussion in our student group because now I could suggest the thesis that the establishment of world law may be a prerequisite to the establishment of a permanent peace, and I could remind them of the difficulties faced by our American forefathers until they discarded the Articles of Confederation in favor of a federation. Some time later, when the discussion group concluded that world federation appeared to be the best approach to a lasting peace, I was happy to agree.

Paris in the spring of 1940 was beautiful, indeed, in spite of the protective sandbagging of statues and historical monuments and the gaping trenches in large grass plots and in parks where air-raid shelters were being constructed. The neatly trimmed trees with tender green leaves were in perfect lines paralleling the avenues, and the flowers in the formal gardens were as beautifully arranged and as colorful as ever. The two-thousand-year-old city, which had hidden the scars of war many times in the past, was now hiding with dignity and charm her fears of the invasion that was sure to come.

After dark, *la ville lumière* became a mammoth ghost town. The metro and the buses closed shop early in the evening. Taxi drivers, whose cab headlights were painted blue during the war, hesitated to venture out at night. The massive utility vehicles, parked overnight in the center of the Avenue des Champs Elysées and other broad avenues, to prevent surprise enemy landings in the heart of the city, suddenly appeared out of the shadowy darkness like threatening Wagnerian phantoms. The darkened windows of the buildings and the black funereal shades wrapped around the street lamps, whose dim light was cast in huge circles on the ground, gave the city a lugubrious atmosphere more suited to a funeral procession slowly marching to the rhythm of Chopin's "Marche Funèbre." It reminded me of a funeral procession I had witnessed in 1929, when the clouds temporarily hid the sun and darkened the streets as the body of Marshal Foch, the victorious commander-in-chief of the Allied armies of World War I, was carried to its resting place in Les Invalides, where Napoleon and other great military heroes rest in peace.

Persons who stayed out after ten or eleven o'clock at night had to walk home. On moonlit nights they listened for Nazi bombers but kept their eyes on the shadows. Walking home alone late one night during the first week of May 1940, I was stopped in the darkness by a man speaking French with a heavy accent which I judged to be either Alsatian or German. It seemed strange to me that he would ask for directions to the City Hall at that hour of the night, but I figured that the City Hall was about as good a place as I could send him, so I gave him correct directions and continued on my way.

At 5:30 a.m., May 10, 1940, the long-awaited Nazi offensive

began with a surprise attack across the neutral borders of Belgium, Holland, and Luxembourg. The main thrust was spearheaded by panzer divisions through Luxembourg toward Sedan at the western end of the Maginot Line, where my friend had spent so much time digging trenches. In less than a week Holland had been split, and Rotterdam heavily bombed, the Netherlands laid down arms, and the panzers crossed the Meuse near Sedan. In Britain, Chamberlain had resigned as prime minister and Churchill took over, offering only "blood, toil, tears, and sweat in a war to the finish."

In Paris we eagerly read the newspapers from cover to cover, searching for any comment that might help us to understand what was really happening. It seemed obvious that more troops and tanks were needed in the north, but we knew that France could ill afford to pull troops away from its southern border as long as "neutral" Italy, which, according to some reports, was still being supplied by American industry, continued to threaten France.

We were astounded at the extent of Nazi superiority in the air and at their ingenuity in using planes at night to drop, along selected routes, French-speaking Nazi men and women dressed as priests and nuns, whose mission was to warn the people that the Nazis were very near and advise them to get out before it was too late. When the French troops tried to advance, they found the roads already blocked by their own people.

About the third day of the offensive, I went to the Gare Saint Lazare to volunteer my services. When the first train from the front came in, I decided to observe in order to determine where I could best serve. I was surprised to see so many bullet holes in the sides of the passenger cars and to hear the engineer complaining that there wasn't a machine gun on the train to help drive off enemy planes. The first passengers to descend were a man and his wife with two children. They had apparently left home hurriedly. The man was carrying a little girl on one arm and a bundle under the other. The woman had a bundle under her arm and was leading a small boy by the hand. The boy was wearing a pullover sweater which stopped just below his navel. That was all he had on.

When all the passengers had descended, I followed them into the station and soon came to a bottleneck which had formed around the metro entrance. Suddenly I realized that I had found my niche. I pushed my way through the crowd to the metro map just outside the metro entrance, approached the man nearest to the map, and asked if I could help him. As soon as I had given him the directions he needed, he left and others approached with their questions. Within an hour the bottleneck was cleared, and I went out to buy a meter stick to help me point out locations near the top of the map when the next train came in.

When it was revealed, May 21, 1940, that the Nazis were within sixty miles of Paris, the evacuation of the city began. Incidentally, among the first to disappear were the refugees who had so mysteriously appeared in the Latin Quarter in the fall of '39. Robert and I did not really feel an urgency to leave Paris, however, until the first week of June after King Leopold of Belgium surrendered and the British were driven from Dunkirk. We were then, of course, fully aware that all the Nazi forces in the north could be turned on Paris. On June 3, when Nazi bombs were dropped on Paris for the first time, I wondered if Adolf the "artiste" was going to renege on his boast that he would "take Paris as one plucks a beautiful rose."

At this time Mr. Williams packed his car so he would be ready to leave on a moment's notice. After leaving Paris he would then have to stop in the country to gather his family before continuing to the Spanish border. Edmond Pendleton, organist and choir director at the American Church, being a bachelor with no family in France to worry about, decided to stay in Paris and continue church services as best he could.

From a business point of view, I knew that Robert should remain in Paris as long as it was safe to do so. With his family already safely settled in a villa at Hendaye Plage at the Spanish border, I figured that Robert and I should be able to remain in Paris as long as the French government did. Robert's reasoning was apparently similar to mine. He had already made arrangements to telephone a friend in government service each morning. When he could not reach his friend, he would know that the government had moved.

Robert and I had already packed several small room-sized sections of Bedel's Storage Warehouse with beautiful Limoges china and handsome house furnishings which he had collected over the years. He had also telephoned to have his Model A Ford, which had been in storage for nine years, taken off the blocks and made ready to use. It ran like a top. Robert was still putting in full-time at his office each day and gradually placing his clients' files in small metal trunks which we planned to take with us when we left.

One night after counting his metal trunks, he stopped at a garage and asked the "garagiste" if he had any large secondhand cars for sale.

The "garagiste" replied, "Oui, monsieur, j'en ai deux."

"May I see them?" Robert asked.

"Mais non, monsieur," came the quick response, "c'est la guerre. Il n'y a pas de lumiére." Then, on second thought, he added, "Elles sont la-bàs au fond, si vous voulez les toucher."

Robert groped his way to the back of the garage and found the two cars. He raised the hood of one of the cars and immediately felt a big hole in a rubber hose leading to the radiator. He turned to the second car and ran his hand over the top of it. It was covered with a thick layer of dust, but beneath the dust he could feel an exceptionally smooth finish. He raised the hood and the parts of the motor he touched felt relatively clean and free of dust. The second car turned out to be an old model black Cadillac limousine whose chauffeur had kept it in excellent repair. Robert bargained with the "garagiste" and bought the car subject to its being cleaned and made ready for use, including a full tank of gas, by noon the following day.

On the night of June 8, 1940, Mr. Williams' brother-in-law, Maurice Bourgin, a French medical officer, arrived with a young French soldier at Mr. Williams's apartment. They had been separated from their outfit, which had been split and scattered by continuous strafing from Nazi planes. The two had caught a train to Paris and planned to leave on an early morning train the next day for Chateau Thierry, where they hoped to rejoin their outfit. What they wanted now was a hot bath and a good night's sleep. Mr. Williams having already left Paris, I let them in the apartment, told them that I would wake them in the morning, and said we would have breakfast together. Then I went to a neighborhood store and bought what I, an American, thought they needed for breakfast.

Since I could think of no better alarm clock than the aroma of hot perking coffee and cooking bacon, I slipped into the apartment about fifteen minutes early, put on the coffee, and started the bacon on low heat while I broke eight eggs in a bowl, salted, peppered, and beat them, because I was sure I knew how to prepare scrambled eggs. Just as I finished taking up the bacon, the two arrived in uniform. Maurice set the table, and the young soldier prepared the toast while I cooked the eggs. Breakfast was served.

I did not have to ask any questions to know how much the time spent at the breakfast table that morning meant to them, and I had only to glance at their plates to know that the "chef's" efforts were appreciated. As they got up to leave Maurice asked, "Jim, do you think France has a chance?" I did not know what to say, so I just thought out loud, "Both of you know the situation you left at the front yesterday, and now you are rushing to rejoin your outfit. With men like you, France will always have a chance." Two days later I learned that Chateau Thierry had fallen.

The next day, June 9, 1940, Nazi tanks were reported thirty-five miles from Paris. On the morning of June 10, Robert's telephone call to his friend in government service revealed that the French government had left Paris. The news announcement during the day that Italy would consider itself at war with France and Britain as of the following morning was a clear signal that the battle for France was now coming to an end.

Few things angered the French more than the role taken by Italy during the war. Under the guise of neutrality, Italy had collaborated with the Nazis while threatening France, thus forcing her to keep a well-equipped army in the south at a time when it was so badly needed in the north. As one Frenchman put it, "Now that France has been beaten to her knees, brave Benito is going to send in his troops to stab us in the back."

After dark that evening, I drove the Model A, with two bicycles strapped on the rear, up the Champs Elysées. As I turned onto the sidewalk, I smiled and nodded to a policeman, who returned the gesture with a salute and watched me as I turned around on the broad sidewalk and backed up to the entrance of number 44. Robert and I spent most of the night packing the remaining files, putting locks on the metal trunks, and taking them down one at a time on the elevator. The elevator was sturdy enough but resembled a delicate little bird cage hanging by one small cable which raised and lowered it up and down the center of an open spiral stairway. We stacked the trunks in the back of the Ford using all the space behind the front seat.

Chapter IV

The eleventh day of June 1940 was perhaps the longest day of my life. We had worked all night, and when we had left the building early that morning, we were told that the Nazis were approaching the suburbs of Paris. I had gotten no sleep, and now at 9:00 a.m. I had just gulped a hasty breakfast and was standing on the sidewalk in front of 65 Quai d'Orsay, waiting for Robert to pick me up. According to our plan, Robert, driving the Cadillac, would get his secretary, Mlle. Doyen, while Mr. David, who worked around the office for Robert, would drive the Ford to make a final check at the office, where they would meet. Then they would drive by 65 Quai d'Orsay to get me on their way out of the city.

At ten o'clock I was still waiting. By eleven o'clock I had gotten tired of standing on the sidewalk and walking back and forth, so I went back inside and up to the library lounge, where I placed a comfortable chair by the window in order to see them when they arrived. Twelve o'clock came and I still could not figure out what could detain them so long. I knew that Mlle. Doyen was not feeling well. She had been through a similar frightening experience in World War I when she was driven from her home in Belgium by the Kaiser's troops. I knew also that if she were ill, Robert would not leave her without first placing her under a doctor's care or taking her to a hospital. At one o'clock I began to get hungry, and I wondered if, for some valid reason, they had stopped to get something to eat before coming by for me. By two o'clock I was beginning to worry about everything, how far the Nazis had advanced during the morning, the conditions of the old Cadillac limousine and the Model A Ford that had been in storage for nine years. Yet I remained absolutely confident that Robert Lee Humber would show up, even if much later than he had originally planned. I am no longer certain of the exact hour of their arrival, but I think it was just before three o'clock that I saw the Cadillac, followed by the Model A, stop in front of the building.

When I stepped out of the building onto the sidewalk, I saw that there were several people in the Cadillac. Robert, who was driving the car, pointed at the Model A and said "Follow me." I quickly got into the Ford, stepped on the starter, and was listening to the beautiful hum of the motor, when I realized that I was not alone. I glanced to my right and had the pleasant surprise of seeing Miss Kitty Kieland, an attractive, petite blond of Scandinavian extraction whom I had seen several times in the church house attending some of our programs. As we drove out of Paris, she explained the delay and how she happened to be with us.

Mlle. Doyen had been quite ill and hadn't even gotten out of bed. Robert needed someone to help get her up. Mr. David, on whom Robert was counting to bring his mother-in-law, Madame Berthier, back to Paris after things settled down, did not want to leave his English girlfriend behind, so he got her' and Kitty, who was then alone and did not know what to do, and brought them, packed and ready to travel, to Mlle. Doyen's apartment. They spent an hour or so persuading her to get up and then helping her to pack. When they stopped to pick me up, Mr. David, who had been driving the Ford, changed to the Cadillac in order to be with his girlfriend.

We hadn't driven many miles from Paris before we became a part of a long line of slow-moving traffic headed southwest. Just before arriving at the town of Etampes the line came to a halt. A series of starts and stops continued until we reached a woods just outside the town. We stayed there for some time. Hidden in the woods were a number of French tanks headed toward Paris. As we drove bumper-to-bumper through Etampes, we had to make a detour which probably indicated that we were circling an area which had been bombed. We did not know, and we certainly did not get out of line and stop to inquire. Getting back into the line of traffic could be quite an ordeal. The trip to Blois was bumper-to-bumper most of the time and very slow.

When we arrived at Blois (177 Km from Paris) late at night, we turned out of the line of traffic and went directly to a service station with which we were familiar on the street paralleling the Loire river. It was owned by an American doughboy and his French wife. Their son, who, incidentally, spoke very

43

little English, greeted us and wanted to help us, but it was late at night, and he was sure that there was not a vacant room in the town. Furthermore, he had sold completely out of gasoline. Fortunately we were able to buy some filling station snacks and drinks which made up our supper.

Finally the young man explained that the gasoline tank farm was on the edge of town and that their tank trucks would supply him early in the morning but he doubted that they would be able to supply stations on the highway. Then he offered to let us park beside the pumps so we would be the first in line in the morning, but he warned that he would not be allowed to sell more than ten liters of gasoline per car. We wasted no time in accepting his offer and placing the cars beside the pumps. I was tired and ready to get some sleep even if I did have to get it draped over a steering wheel.

Early the next morning, while the tank truck was supplying the filling station with gasoline, we filled our arms with snacks and drinks because we did not know when, where, or even if we would get a warm meal any time soon. Then we took on our twenty liters of gasoline and started out, without even slowing down to bid farewell to the historic Chateau de Blois, whose replica Cornelius Vanderbilt constructed in the beautiful setting of Biltmore in the mountains of North Carolina.

Assuming that the French government had moved southwest away from the approaching Nazi army, and relocated at Tours, we decided to cross the Loire river at Blois, thus avoiding Tours, its traffic, and its bridge, which could be destroyed. Our destination for the day was Angoulème, where Robert wanted to stop long enough to speak to his brother-in-law, André Berthier, who was working there during the war as a chemist. After a long day of tense, uneven driving, during which there was rarely an opportunity to relax, we arrived at Angoulème at dusk in a yellowish smog. André came out to greet us and give us directions to a football field some distance away where people who wanted to stop for the night were being advised to go. We were happy to get away from the plant whose peculiar smog was beginning to irritate our throats and make us want to cough. When we reached the football field there were a number of cars already parked. We drove to a spot near an exit and parked for the night.

June 13, 1940, the day we drove from Angoulème to Bordeaux, was also the day that Winston Churchill flew to Tours, where the French asked if Britain would release them from their pledge not to seek a separate peace. Churchill replied that he could not, but he added that he understood France's predicament.

We arrived at Bordeaux during the afternoon and drove immediately to the big open square in the center of the city, where we parked our cars and got our first and only hot meal during our five-day trip from Paris to Hendaye.

Bordeaux was a hotbed of rumors, making it virtually impossible to separate fact from fiction. The rumors ran something like this: "Having just been through a civil war, Spain does not have adequate provisions to feed all the refugees entering the country. Refugees leaving automobiles in Lisbon are undermining the Portuguese automobile business. Spain is sympathetic to the Nazis and may very well join them as Italy did. Nazi officials are already in Spain. The French government will relocate from Tours to Bordeaux tomorrow."

There were no vacant rooms in Bordeaux that night, other than possibly those being reserved for French government officials rumored to arrive during the night or the next morning. But we had our uncomfortable bedrooms out there among the hundreds of other uncomfortable four-wheel bedrooms, parked in that huge square in the heart of the city, where we were destined to spend a restless night with our car windows at least partially open among all those people getting in and out of their cars, walking back and forth among the cars most of the night. There was such confusion, I could hardly remember whether I draped my arms over the steering wheel or through the spokes of the wheel to get a comfortable position before going to sleep. About the time I got settled, the air-raid siren wailed and wailed until everybody was awake and stirring again. I said to myself, "This is no place to be." But how to get out of that mass of cars and people without turning on headlights and who would dare turn on headlights during an air-raid alert: I knew that Robert was anxious to be with his family, especially since Lucie had recently told him that Aileen, their one-and-a-half-year-old infant daughter, was ill. An hour or so later things quieted down again, but when the first light of dawn appeared, people began cranking up and moving out and so did we. At least one of the rumors of the night before was correct. It was indeed the next day, June 14, 1940, that the French government relocated from Tours to Bordeaux. It was also on that day that the French prime minister, Paul Reynaud, informed President Roosevelt of the imminent fall of France and appealed to him to enter the war.

As we drove through Les Landes, a large flat, pine forest area south of Bordeaux, it began to rain, and almost immediately I began to laugh. Kitty, of course, wanted to know what on earth I saw to laugh about. "Did you see that road we just passed on the right with the sign pointing to Mimizan?" I said. "Well, eleven years ago, I was bicycling alone from Paris to Hendaye and on this very stretch of road I got caught in a rain storm. The wide ditches beside the road filled with water and prevented me from seeking shelter among the trees, so, since I was already wet, I decided to continue riding in the rain. After awhile a Frenchman drove up beside me, lowered his car window, looked at me and then, pointing at the sky, he shouted, 'Il pleut.' With the number of people in his car it was obvious that he was not planning to give me a lift but just having some fun at my expense.

"As if I weren't aware of his prank or of the rain, I took my right hand off the handgrip, turned it palm upward toward the sky, quickly caught some of the pouring rain in the cup of my hand and watched the water very closely as I poured it out of my hand. Then, with a silly openmouthed grin on my face, I looked back at the man, pointed at the sky, and replied in a thick, stupid voice, 'Oui, il pleut.' The Frenchman looked back at me as if he wasn't sure whether I was kidding or not. I laughed and waved to him as he quickly ran up his window and sped away. I didn't stop laughing until I came to that Mimizan sign. There, I turned off and followed that road more than an hour before I arrived at Mimizan Plage, where I stripped to my shorts and got a good sunbath on the beautiful sandy beach while my clothes were drying."

I was glad this time that I was not on a bicycle, because the rain did not let up. Just before dark it rained so hard we could hardly see the road. Robert finally spotted a wide driveway on the right and turned in. I followed and stopped beside him. We did not know where we were, but early the next morning when I woke up, I understood why the driveway was so wide. We were parked in the entrance to a fire station. Without thanking our host that fifteenth day of June 1940, we quietly backed out and continued our journey south. As we passed through Bayonne, we saw men crowding on fishing boats which were preparing to sail around the Brittany peninsula to England to join the French troops who had escaped across the

Channel at Dunkirk.

When we reached Hendaye Plage, we stopped at the Hotel Liliac, a small hotel where Mr. David and the ladies were able to get lodging; then Robert and I continued to an oceanfront villa next door to Aéten Etchea, the villa which Robert had rented for his family vacation the summer before. When we arrived, Lucie took Robert by the hand and led him into the house, where she revealed the heartrending news of the death of their infant daughter, Aileen. During the next few days Lucie and Robert stayed close together. Aileen was buried in a temporary grave in the Hendaye Cemetery. After the war, Robert and his family returned to France and had the body of Aileen Geneviève Humber moved to the Berthier family plot at Villeneuve-Saint-Georges just outside of Paris.

On the sixteenth of June 1940 a message from President Roosevelt put an end to Prime Minister Reynaud's hopes for American intervention. Reynaud resigned and Marshal Pétain was asked to form a government. On the seventeenth of June 1940 Marshal Pétain asked the Spanish ambassador to approach the Germans concerning an armistice. Two days later, on June 19, 1940, Francisco Franco offered to join the war with the Axis powers if Spain were given British Gibraltar and French Morocco. On the twenty-first of June the Nazis read the terms of the proposed armistice to French representatives at Compiègne in the same railroad car in which the Germans had signed the armistice ending World War I. Two days later, on June 23, Robert asked Mr. David to place the Ford in the line of cars approaching the international bridge in order to hold a place for the Cadillac. This maneuver gave Lucie and the boys more time with Mme. Berthier before leaving France. Of course, Mr. David or someone had to stay in the car at all times to keep from losing the place when the line advanced. The next day, June 24, when we came back to check the line we found that the Ford had advanced less than half the distance to the bridge. Meanwhile, word was spreading that the cease-fire which Marshal Pétain was seeking would be announced at any moment. We knew that if we did not pass through the French frontier barrier at the bridge before the cease-fire, we could find ourselves at the mercy of the Nazis.

On the rainy morning of June 25, 1940, when the Cadillac replaced the Ford in the line, we were still some distance from the bridge. Late in the morning, however, things began to happen as the news was circulated that the cease-fire had been agreed upon and would go into effect without delay. Immediately café and restaurant owners moved all their chairs and tables on the sidewalks inside because they knew that many French people did not approve of the cease-fire and they feared trouble. People in the line of cars approaching the bridge over the Bidoassa, which separates France from Spain at that point, became afraid to wait any longer. Some of them had their baggage carried to the Spanish frontier barrier at the other end of the bridge, while they got rid of their cars. Then they walked across the bridge. One chauffeur was given two cars which, in all probability, since no gasoline would be available to him, he would have to store for the duration of the war unless the Nazis relieved him of his problem. During all this activity the line advanced less slowly. As we reached the French frontier barrier we bade farewell to our friends who had come in the driving rain to see us off. Then we drove onto the bridge where, to our surprise, we faced new developments and new problems.

As if to relieve us of our worries, two men approached, saying that they were representatives of the American Embassy and had come to get our passports which they would take back to Bordeaux in order to get for us the newly required appropriate visa. Frankly, under the circumstances, I did not like the idea of giving up my passport and becoming a person without identity and without a country even for a half a day. Then they repeated to us the explanation which they had probably just given a dozen times on the bridge ahead of us.

Apparently the Portuguese government had just decided not to admit anyone into Portugal who did not have passage on a steamer leaving the country. We had our tickets, but Spain, in turn, had decided to admit only those who had the new visa to Portugal. When they showed us their briefcase full of passports, we gave them ours. We were going south fleeing the Nazis but sending our passports north back toward the Nazis. It was not very comforting and neither were the wind-blown showers which kept us sitting in the car while we slowly advanced a few feet at the time.

Later in the afternoon, the same afternoon that Marshal Pétain laid down arms, the line of cars inching their way across the bridge toward Spain stopped moving altogether. We had not reached the halfway point on the bridge, our passports had not been returned, and apparently the Spanish customs officials had quit work for the day. I couldn't help but wonder if they would have put in a little overtime if their country had been more sympathetic to the cause of freedom for all men. Then, on second thought, I wondered how many Americans who enjoy the privilege of living in a democratic country are aware of the urgency of extending that freedom to all men throughout the world as rapidly as they become able and willing to accept the responsibilities encumbent upon free men everywhere.

It was turning dark, and I was buried in thought when the embassy officials arrived with our passports. There was one for everybody in the car except Robert. His was not among those remaining, but one of the officials remembered having called out Robert's name. After backtracking, they found his passport in the hand of a drunk who had already placed his passport picture over Robert's.

Now with no new problems facing us and my passport in hand I decided to give Robert and Lucie and the two boys a little time to themselves. I put on my rain gear and stepped out into the blustery weather.

As I walked toward the Spanish end of the bridge, the rainy weather was cold and disagreeable, and the wind was terribly annoying until I met someone who told me that the storm we were experiencing was the remnant of a hurricane that had skirted the coast of North Carolina before crossing the Atlantic. Suddenly the wind and rain seemed playful rather than annoying. I threw back my hood, took off my glasses, and let the rain beat on my face. The water was invigorating, and it even seemed to have a light taste of salt like the water I remembered tasting in the 1933 hurricane which blew part of the roof off the Atlantic Beach Hotel on Bogue Banks and dug a hole more than six feet deep in the sand at the northwest corner of the Seashore Club, where I was visiting Robert H. Wright, president of East Carolina Teachers College and his family at the time. The gusting winds shaking the cars on the international bridge were bringing me a real Outer Banks welcome, and I was enjoying it thoroughly. The people in the cars nearby temporarily forgot their troubles as they watched me and laughed.

When I reached the Spanish end of the bridge, I picked up a conversation in French with a young Polish refugee who had managed to stay ahead of the Nazis across Europe to that

49

point. He did not have the necessary papers to enter Spain. While talking to him I noticed a group of ladies who had left their car and walked across the bridge during the afternoon. They had apparently gotten through customs before they closed and were now standing in the rain by their baggage not more than twenty feet from us on the other side of the barrier. I assumed that they were waiting for transportation, so I told the Polish refugee, who did not speak English, what I would do if he wanted me to. He looked at me and said, "Oui, merci beaucoup." Then I moved to one side so I would be facing the ladies, yet apparently speaking to the young man. Raising my voice slightly, I said to him in English, "I am sure those ladies would appreciate your helping with their luggage when their bus arrives." One of the ladies turned and looked at me, then at him, and smiled. I hope he made it. I think he was a Jew. I don't believe he would have lasted long with the Nazis.

As I started walking back across the bridge, I saw a number of people I had met in Paris over the years, and I stopped to speak to a few of them. When I came to Dr. Horatio S. Krans, who was director of the American University Union in Paris, I went around to the lee side of his car to talk with him and Mrs. Krans for awhile. It was Dr. Krans who helped me to get a scholarship in 1928 which gave me a year as "assistant d'anglais" at Valence. They had ample room in their car for me to ride with them and if I had thought that they needed me, I would have shifted to their car. As it turned out, I was more help to Robert in his antique Cadillac limousine than I would have been to them.

When I reached the midway point of the bridge I stopped to see who had made it to that point before the Spanish customs officials stopped work in the afternoon. There I saw a small low-slung British roadster with two men squeezed in it. As I approached, one of them got out of the car and stood in the rain to smoke a cigarette. He was a chain-smoker whom we all know and admire and whom I was happy to see some years later when he came to East Carolina University in Greenville, North Carolina, to give our commencement address. It was Edward R. Murrow. After walking past about six more cars, I came to Robert's tall black Cadillac limousine. I quietly opened the door, stepped up into the car, and was soon sound asleep.

The next morning, June 26, it was almost ten o'clock before the cars ahead of us had left the bridge and it was our turn.

We had not driven more than two miles in Spain when we met two official Mercedes-Benz limousines, flying Nazi swastikas, headed toward the bridge. Thus, another rumor heard at Bordeaux turned out to be fact rather than fiction.

The Spanish customs officials at the bridge had told us what route to follow across Spain to Portugal but upon studying the map, we saw that another route was considerably shorter, so we took the shorter route. We had traveled only two days in Spain when the right rear tire of the old limousine went flat and our problems began again. We knew that we would have difficulty finding a tire to fit the tall, narrow wheels of a car of that vintage. Robert telephoned ahead to try to locate a tire that would fit, while I started jacking up the heavily loaded car. When he returned with no tire, we decided to stuff the flat tire with ferns, leaves, and rags and go as far as we could, then try again to locate a suitable tire. Suffice it to say that our trip across Spain was slow and lumbering.

We arrived at the Portuguese frontier on July 11 and immediately were told by an American Embassy official that he had just been advised that an order was on its way to Spanish border officials to detain any refugees who had not followed the designated route across Spain. Having this information was very important to us. It enabled the embassy officials and others to press for a speedy customs inspection, which permitted us to enter Portugal before the order reached the border officials.

When we drove onto the wharf at Lisbon, the handsome black Cadillac limousine was quickly unloaded and the contents placed on board the *Manhattan* which sailed the next day, Friday, July 12, at 5:35 p.m., on what her crew thought would be her last voyage across the Atlantic before being converted into a United States troopship. Robert satisfied the Portuguese demand that automobiles not be abandoned in Portugal by presenting "la belle dame noire d'un certain age" to the American Embassy. We arrived in New York on the afternoon of July 18, 1940.

Chapter V

The return of Robert Lee Humber to his home in Greenville, North Carolina, completed a long cycle of preparation for his lifework. Early in his youth he learned to set goals high enough to be worthy of his best effort. In his preteen years he decided that he wanted to become a Rhodes scholar, and he willingly accepted the necessity of riding his bicycle twelve miles weekly to an academy in Winterville in order to meet the Rhodes Scholarship requirement of two years of Latin before entering college. During his years of study for his A.B. and L.L.B. degrees at Wake Forest College, his M.A. at Harvard University, and his B. Litt. as a Rhodes Scholar at New College, Oxford, Robert Lee Humber followed a broad liberal arts curriculum with some emphasis on history, law, and government. His experience as a young artillery officer in World War I reinforced his belief that war is a horrible waste which settles no problems. In Rome in 1921, while sitting at the foot of the Temple of Julius Caesar, contemplating the remains of triumphal arches that were erected to commemorate the victories of the Roman emperors, Robert reflected upon man's struggle through the ages to establish peace on earth, and while there in the Roman Forum he pledged to do all in his power to make a serious contribution to modern man's search for world peace.

On April 25, 1921, just a little more than one month before his twenty-third birthday, he wrote to my sister Louise: "World empires before have been thought of and attempted, but they have been maintained only at the point of the bayonet. Instead of the bayonet there now must be substituted the ballot. Centralized despotisms dictated the policies of the ancient empires, but the new world government must be controlled solely by the expressed will of the people. The old organizations were the results purely of personal am-

52

bition; the new organization must be the result of humanity struggling to give vent to its universal sympathies, the consolidation of her mutual interests. Liberty, not individual tyranny, must be its cornerstone."

From Rome Robert continued his travels to Athens, Cairo, Bombay, Calcutta, and through the Orient to America, stopping for a short visit with his brother, Dr. John Davis Humber, a surgeon in San Francisco, and for a short stay at home in Greenville, North Carolina, before returning to Oxford. After completing his bachelor of literature degree at Oxford, he could not resist the challenge of France and Paris, the crossroads of western civilization. Once in Paris, he did not seek the Doctorat de l'Université, which he probably could have obtained in two or three years; he chose the highest degree that the French nation offers, the Doctorat de l'Etat, which usually requires from six to ten years of diligent research and writing.

On May 31, 1929, in a letter to my mother, he wrote: "At this moment, I still have one chapter and a conclusion to write, after which I must give about six weeks of time to unifying and amplifying the text of my volume, which will probably be about 450 or more pages. I then will have to translate it into French and to supervise its publication. Dr. Jamieson, the chief of the manuscript department of the Congressional Library, has just sent me copies of about eighty-seven unpublished letters of Calhoun, which I propose to edit and publish as my second thesis."

Since graduating from Wake Forest College in 1918, Robert Lee Humber had supported himself through scholarships and tutoring. Now, in 1929, tutoring was taking too much time away from his studies. He told me one day of his conversation with Mr. Strassburger of Philadelphia, who wanted him to tutor his son, Peter. Robert liked Mr. Strassburger and his son, but he did not want any more students. Mr. Strassburger, however, had decided that Robert was the man he wanted to tutor his son and continued to insist. Finally, thinking he would end the conversation, Robert said, "No one would pay what I would ask to take on another student at this time." Mr. Strassburger said, "And what would you ask?" Robert told him and Mr. Strassburger replied, "Can you start right away?"

Another person whom Robert was tutoring at the time was

destined to change the immediate objective of his endeavors and finally to put an end to his tutoring years. This man was Thomas Gilcrease of Tulsa, Oklahoma. At twenty-one years of age, Thomas Gilcrease was called to the family attorney's office and told that he had inherited valuable oil land. The attorney then gave him some fatherly advice saying, "Tom, you can sell this land today and tomorrow you will be a millionaire, but your life will be over. On the other hand, you can keep this land and through toil and sweat you can build your own company and have the fight of your life, because they will surely try to take it away from you."

After twenty years of toil and sweat Thomas Gilcrease, who had built a small oil company, valued in 1929 at approximately three million dollars, decided that it was time for him to learn something about the world which he had never taken the time to see. He and his young wife (his first wife had died) took their infant daughter, Dacine, to Paris, where they settled in an apartment on the Right Bank, a short distance from the Pont de l'Alma.

When Tom sought a tutor of French history, he was referred to Robert Lee Humber. Within a very short time the two men developed great respect for one another. Robert liked Tom's frankness and honesty, and Tom learned very quickly that Robert was a man of strong character, with an incredible store of knowledge not only in the fields of history and literature, but in many fields including the exact science of mathematics.

One day as Robert was talking to Tom about a problem that Napoleon had faced and of the decision he had reached, Tom exclaimed, "If I had known that ten years ago it would have saved me thousands of dollars." Robert asked what the circumstances were. Tom described the situation and without a moment's hesitation Robert explained that under the laws of the state of Texas he should have done thus and so. From that moment Tom kept the subject of conversation on the small American oil company. He explained to Robert that the big oil companies which owned the refineries literally held the small operators over the barrel. They would pay only one dollar a barrel for crude oil. At that rate even a company which owned considerable acreage of good oil land could grow only at a snail's pace unless it was willing to bury itself in high-risk indebtedness.

Tom then asked Robert if he would accompany him to some

European refineries to see if he could make a better deal with one of them. Robert agreed, and they visited one refinery in the Netherlands and one in France. When they returned to Paris they were very optimistic. It appeared that they would be successful. But that was in the year 1929, and they did not foresee the stock market crash. When President Roosevelt closed the banks and the United States went off the gold standard, international negotiation of this type came to an abrupt halt.

Tom, however, was not discouraged. He had seen Robert move smoothly and convincingly in business circles, and now he was ready to make a new proposal. He would establish a European headquarters of the Gilcrease Oil Company in Paris for the purpose of selling stock in the company so as to bring in the steady flow of cash needed to enable the company to speed up its production and growth, if Robert would assume responsibility for planning, organizing, and directing the European operation.

Robert's religious and moral bias steered him away from the sale of stock which could be placed on the market and used for gambling purposes. He changed the stock into partnership agreements in which the investor and the company would share equally in the profits of each deal. Then, after two trips to America to study the company, see its holdings, and question its officers and its attorney, he accepted Tom's offer, explaining to him that he had taken so much time reaching his decision because he did not want to ask others to invest their money unless he was willing to invest his own. Then he requested that his commissions be invested in the same manner as the investments of his clients.

During one of his trips to America, Robert stopped in Washington, D.C. long enough to discuss with Secretary of State Cordell Hull problems facing the American Church in Paris which had been brought on by the depression and French taxes. He asked the secretary of state if he would propose a treaty with France exempting from taxation American churches located in France and exempting from American taxation French churches in America. Secretary Hull told Robert that he was the first man to ask him to draw up a treaty in order to get out of taxes. They both enjoyed a good laugh and the treaty was drafted.

The handsomely appointed offices selected in Paris occupied the entire top floor of 44 Avenue des Champs Elysées. Each office opened through French doors onto a broad terrace over-looking the avenue, giving a magnificent view from the Arc de Triomphe at the top of the hill to the Place de la Concorde at the foot of the hill. As the executive officer, Robert was to plan, organize, and direct the entire European operation of the company and serve as its legal council.

Meanwhile the depression of 1930 caught up with me, and I made plans to return to America to do that which I thought I was then best prepared to do to teach French. I had spent three years in France, the first in Paris as a student of the language, including the study of phonetics and voice lessons. One of the first lessons I learned in France, however, was a lesson in maturity given to me by a French taxi driver at a time when I had been in France less than five months. It was in late 1927 when there were few stoplights and French taxi drivers seemed to know only three things about a car: the horn, the accelerator, and the brake. I hailed a cab on the Quai d'Orsay, told the driver where I wanted to go and started to sit down. I hit the back of the seat just after the accelerator hit the floor. We had only about four blocks to go before making a right turn onto the Pont de l'Alma. As we approached the corner I saw a taxi on our left coming at breakneck speed toward the same corner. Neither driver would put on brakes until the very last second. As we came to a halt the taxi on our left lightly tapped our left rear fender. My driver got out and started giving the driver of the other cab a lecture. The other driver, who didn't appreciate being told how to drive, called my driver every ugly name he could think of in and out of the dictionary. Finally my driver got back in his cab, the other driver backed his cab about an inch, and we drove off. When I got to my destination and paid my driver I said to him, "You were right back at the bridge. The other driver was completely wrong, yet he called you everything ugly he could think of. I was expecting you to knock his block off." My driver looked at me astounded. Making a gesture with his fist he said, "The first man to pass a lick admits defeat." From that moment, I knew that I wanted to know more about France and the French people.

I completed my studies at the Alliance Française, receiving the *Diplôme superieur d'études françaises modernes,* and spent my second year on scholarship as "assistant d'anglais at the Ecole Normale de Valence. I used my Christmas holidays to see the Roman monuments of Avignon, Arles, and Nîmes and went on to visit Monaco and the Riviera to the Italian border. Then I returned to school through the Alps on a narrow-gauge railroad in a two-car train, making frequent stops to pick up children going back to school and also a few unscheduled stops to give the little engine time to build up more steam when the climb was too steep and the snow too deep. The third year I went back to Paris to continue my studies of the French language and literature. During those three years I traveled over most of France by train, automobile, and bicycle, stopping to visit the most outstanding monuments, chateaux, and other places of interest.

On one bicycle trip Robert and I covered about one thousand miles in nineteen days zigzagging from Paris to Bordeaux, then turning north to Mont Saint Michel, Bayeux, and Saint Malo, passing through Montesquieu country near Bordeaux, visiting the monastery at Mont Saint Michel, not forgetting to stop for our omlette at Mére Poularde's, examining Mathilda's tapestry at Bayeux, and walking at low tide to visit Chateaubriand's tomb on the little island of Petit Bé off Saint Malo.

The two years that I lived in Paris, during my first trip over, I spent most of my spare time trying to learn as much as possible about French civilization. I spent a great deal of time visiting the historic monuments of Paris and examining the treasures of the Louvre, Cluny, and other museums. Using entertainment available in Paris as stepping stones, I went from an all-Debussy concert played by Maurice Ravel to a visit of the impressionist paintings of Monet while the music was still in my ears; from a concert by the renowned Russian basso profundo Chaliapin to one by the popular Italian tenor Gigli; from the one-thousandth-plus performance of "Rose Marie" to numerous evenings at the opera followed by the traditional *soupe à l'oignon* at Les Halles. From the formal reception of Emil Ludwig to the Academie Française, I went to Saint Julien le Pauvre, where Dante went to pray, and François Villon went to shoot craps. From the beautiful Christmas service at Saint Eustache I went to Saint Sulpice to hear the great organ at which Saint-Saens composed "La Danse macabre," which caused him to be expelled from the church. And, of course, I took in the Davis Cup matches at Auteuil, featuring Jean Barotra—the bounding Basque and one of the most interesting players I have ever seen—and Big

57

Bill Tilden, with his cannonball serve, and René LaCoste representing France.

At a time when tennis was a gentleman's game, our American representative gave the world a preview of the future of the game by losing his composure and taking out his frustration on the ball boys, an act which caused most of the four thousand embarrassed American spectators to shift their applause to his opponent René LaCoste, who became the tournament champion.

One of the most interesting and educational (but time-consuming) attractions in Paris was its café life. Each day as we left our class at the Sorbonne we went to a café on the "Boule Miche" and continued discussion of the professor's topic of the day. I learned very quickly that the French are clear thinkers but very individualistic. Perhaps that explains why there are so many political parties in France. At one time during the late 1920s there were more than twenty political parties, including the communists and the royalists, represented in the Chamber of Deputies and the Senate. This great diversity of political thought in France was not surprising, however, because as early as the eighteenth century the French Age of Reason had a profound influence on the thinking of the people of France and also, incidentally, on the thinking of our founding fathers through Montesquieu and others.

Certain writers, artists, and poets living in Paris frequented certain cafés. One knew, for example, that Picasso would be at the Café de Flore at Saint Germain des Près around 4 p.m. One day, as I was going from "Boale Miche" to Saint Germain des Près, I took a shortcut across a corner of the Luxembourg Gardens. As I passed the Senate House I saw a group of senators playing croquet. Although it was cloudy and looked a bit threatening, I stopped to watch the game. The senators were playing partners, two against two, and appeared to be taking the game quite seriously. The two partners whose turn it was to play took an awfully long time to decide whether they would shoot for the wicket or hit the opponents' ball first. Finally they decided and declared their intention. Then one of the players placed his mallet behind the ball, took aim, and was about to hit the ball when a clap of thunder broke the silence and a pigeon sitting on a limb above dropped a bomb directly in his line of play. The senator looked up and exclaimed, "Un acte de Dieu." Then he turned, repositioned himself behind the ball, and took the alternate shot which they had discussed but had not declared. As soon as he had taken the shot his opponent came over, looked up at the tree limb then down at the ground and said, "Et tu appelles cela un acte de Dieu?" Everybody quickly gathered around in order not to miss a word of what seemed to have the promise of becoming the debate of the century but another "acte," a cloudburst, sent everyone quickly scurrying for shelter. I was tempted to continue in the rain to Saint Germain des Près in order to give Picasso a description of the senators' eventful croquet game. I thought that he could paint a brightly tri-colored Picasso pigeon with one eye pointing aft and the other heavenward, but I couldn't imagine how he would distort the pigeon or the picture enough to reveal the contradictory metaphysicotheological sentiments which flashed through the minds of senators and spectators alike.

The Rotonde, the Dôme, and the Coupole in the Montparnasse area were also great gathering places for students and artists, but when I entered the huge Coupole, I got the impression that I was in the presence of a goodly number of Sisley Hudleston's characters who "tried to hope that they would again try to try."

It was at the Colisée Café on the Champs Elysées that I met Mr. Bunau-Varilla and heard the interesting story of his famous or infamous "Stamp Act of 1902," which shifted U.S. congressional interest in Nicaragua as a potential canal site to Panama. The Walker Commission had recommended Nicaragua as the best route for an Isthmian Canal from the Atlantic to the Pacific. The Panama Canal Company, in which Mr. Bunau-Varilla was interested, had offered to sell its interests in Panama for $109,000,000. A few weeks later a bill introduced in the House of Representatives providing for the construction of a canal through Nicaragua was passed. Whereupon Mr. Bunau-Varilla offered to drop $69,000,000 from his original price if the canal were built in Panama.

Shortly thereafter, the Walker Commission reversed itself, recommending Panama instead of Nicaragua. Apparently, in light of these manipulations, the U.S. Congress simply raised its eyebrows and decided to stick with Nicaragua.

Then in the spring of 1902 the Mont Pélé volcano in Martinique erupted, causing great destruction and loss of life. It reminded Mr. Bunau-Varilla of a stamp, issued by the Nicaraguan government in 1900, depicting the lake of

Nicaragua and the Momotombo volcano to which the artist had added a column of smoke to make the stamp more interesting. A few days before the final vote of Congress on the issue of a choice between Panama and Nicaragua, Mr. Bunau-Varilla located and purchased ninety of those one-cent stamps in Washington, D.C. and sent them to members of Congress, reminding them that there is nothing more authentic than a government stamp. The U.S. Congress selected Panama over Nicaragua by a very narrow margin.

It was also at the Colisée Café that I first met Louis Orr, who years later gave me one of his North Carolina etchings with a note, "to James L. Fleming from the Artiste."

I was lucky to be able to remain in Paris long enough to have the pleasure of serving as best man in Robert and Lucie Humber's wedding, October 16, 1929, and of seeing the Gilcrease Oil Company's European headquarters ready for occupation before I left for America.

I was also very fortunate to be invited to teach French at Guilford College in Greensboro, North Carolina, among some of the finest people I have ever known. I had hardly gotten settled at Guilford when I received a cablegram from Robert telling me that if I had any money that I wanted to invest, to send it to Tom. I remained at Guilford several years and I loved every minute I was there. Deep within me, however, I felt that I had to return to Paris to seek the Doctorat de l'-Université. After receiving my master's from Harvard University in 1937, I returned to Paris where I selected a thesis subject involving a comparative study of the works of O. Henry and those of Guy de Maupassant. I spent more than six months reading in the field before I discovered at the University of Strassbourg a thesis on virtually the same subject written by a Texan. Just when Hitler's war of nerves was becoming a disturbing factor in France, I tried to select a new thesis subject. I did, but I must confess that it never became so interesting to me as the history in the making all around me.

Chapter VI

Soon after Robert Humber and his family were settled in his father's home in Greenville, North Carolina, Mr. Gilcrease called from Tulsa, Oklahoma, offering Robert the presidency of the Gilcrease Oil Company with remuneration equal to that which he himself was receiving from the company at that time. Robert was appreciative of the generous offer and thanked Tom sincerely. He knew, however, that the time had now come when he should actively respond to a greater challenge which he had first sensed at Harvard University following his military service in World War I. He had nurtured this challenge in his heart and mind since 1921, a time of decisions in his life, when he pledged to do all in his power to make a serious contribution to man's search for a permanent world peace. He wrote in a letter to my sister Louise at that time: "The political organization of this world government must be patterned substantially upon the principles of the union of the American states. It must be virile, strong and powerful. . . . I believe the present League of Nations finds historically its counterpart in the Articles of Confederation, which were supplanted by an effectual government because the Articles of Confederation demonstrated their inefficacy through lack of power to achieve."

Now in 1940 the world was at war again and the peace would come. There was no time to lose and so much to be done. Robert had spent many years of his life preparing to meet this very challenge, and he was convinced that he could make a valuable contribution to the search for a lasting peace. He also knew, however, that political theories without political backing die, and he was not at this time a political figure with political backing. He was a scholar who had been away from his native land seventeen years and had just returned home. He could shout his political theories from his rooftop but to what avail? The leading scholars and scientists of the world were already doing just that. On June 22, 1940, as Robert, on his way home from war-torn France, was approaching the Spanish frontier, Albert Einstein was urging the creation of a world federation with military power. Others were making similar statements but the political and military leaders of the world were not listening. They were too busy planning and executing military strategy to think about the details of the peace that would follow the war. Later, they would form a United Nations of twenty-six allied nations to continue the fighting and begin shaping their own plans for peace.

It appeared that the only way to introduce new ideas with any chance of having them heard was through the slow but tried and tested democratic procedure of going first to the grassroots, convincing the people of the validity of the ideas, then soliciting their aid in persuading their representatives to support those ideas. With this procedure in mind, Robert retired to the solitude of his study and began drafting a document which he believed the people and their legislators would understand and support.

About a month and a half later Robert called me into his study, handed me a document, and asked me to read and comment. During the following week he asked two other persons to do the same. A few weeks later, after making some deletions, he took his copy to Edwards and Broughton in Raleigh to have it printed in pamphlet form as a resolution to be presented to the 1941 session of the North Carolina General Assembly. Then, in order to give his grassroots movement for world federation an authentic beginning, he invited some "friends and neighbors" to come to a meeting on Davis Island in Carteret County, North Carolina, on December 27, 1940.

The twenty-seventh of December 1940 was a beautiful clear day, with the temperature in the seventies. Those who went to the island from Greenville, besides Mr. R. L. Humber, Sr., Robert and Lucie Humber and their two boys, Marcel and John, were members of my family: my mother, Mrs. James L. Fleming, Sr.; my younger sister, Margaret F. Winstead; her husband, Dr. John L. Winstead; their two children, John L., Jr., Lou White Winstead; and I. My sister Louise, who was not at home at the time, did not attend. The remainder of the thirty-nine persons who went to the island that day were "friends and neighbors" from Morehead City, Beaufort, and a few communities down east near the island. Robert's uncle and aunt, Mr. and Mrs. M. Leslie Davis of Beaufort, North Carolina, joined us at Smyrna on our way to the island.

After Robert and Lucie had greeted the guests and served them a picnic lunch, Robert lead them to a live oak and holly grove near the shore immediately to the east of the house where folding chairs had been placed. Then, standing a few feet to the east of the front porch, Robert began speaking first of the serenity of the setting on that warm December day. As he looked across Core Sound at Cape Lookout lighthouse in the distance and followed the North Carolina Outer Banks northward to the horizon, he spoke of Roanoke Island, the site of the first English attempt at settling this land, and of Kill Devil Hills, where the Wright brothers made their first successful flight. Then with a twinkle in his eye he said, "Who knows, some day our meeting here today may prove of historical significance." As he turned away from the peaceful beauty of the North Carolina coast to the war that was raging across the Atlantic, almost as if staged, the hunters quietly waiting in the blinds for miles around suddenly started firing their guns as the ducks began to stir. The gun blasts seemed to punctuate Robert's words as he depicted the horror of war and insisted that the peace this time must be won for all mankind.

Following a few comments about the purpose of the meeting on Davis Island, he drew from his pocket a copy of his resolution on world federation and read from it, stopping occasionally to answer questions or to elaborate when he felt it was needed.

When Robert stopped reading, Judge Luther Hamilton of Morehead City rose and said, "When I came here today, I did not know the purpose of this meeting. Now I stand full of pride and joy at being a party to this gathering and excited at the opportunity to offer my support to this resolution." Judge Hamilton concluded his enthusiastic remarks with a motion that the group go on record as favoring the resolution. Two of us seconded the motion simultaneously. Several others spoke briefly. The vote was taken and passed without a dissenting voice, and group discussions followed.

Later in the afternoon, as we left the island, we could still feel the warmth and sincerity of Judge Hamilton's reaction to Robert's presentation of his resolution. Like Judge Hamilton, we all knew that we had been privileged to listen to the sound reasoning of a scholarly gentleman who believed in the brotherhood of man and who sincerely wanted our state and our nation to lead the way to a lasting peace.

The meeting at Davis Island was not sponsored or financed by any organization nor did it mark the birth of an organization. No organization was established; no officers were elected; no funds were solicited or accepted. The meeting at Davis Island was the active beginning of the Robert Lee Humber movement for world federation—a grassroots movement which people joined bearing their own expenses as Robert did, because they believed that world federation was the best approach to a lasting peace, and they wanted to see it realized. The movement thus became a movement of the people, by the people, and for the people—all people—and Robert Lee Humber was its inspirational leader, who chose the tough but sound grassroots approach in order to assure that people would become involved and that world federation would have a chance of becoming, someday, a political reality. He then set an example for those who might join him, carrying the full burden of a hard and determined campaign across the state of North Carolina.

As for me, I had already accepted an invitation to speak to a group of ladies in Farmville, North Carolina, four days later, on December 31, 1940, on the subject they had suggested, our exodus from Paris. I felt, however, that the ladies would not mind my shortening the story of our exodus and talking about world federation. They proved that I was correct in my judgment of them by becoming the first group, following the original meeting on Davis Island, to endorse the resolution. Here is a list of those ladies whose names I was able to obtain following the meeting: Mrs. B. 0. Turnage, hostess; Mrs. J. M. Hobgood, who made the motion to endorse the resolution; Mrs. W. R. Willis of Manteo, who seconded the motion; Mrs. R. A. Fields, program chairman; Mrs. J. G. Thorne; Mrs. A. C. Monk; Mrs. Leroy Rollins; Mrs. J. C. Morgan; Mrs. W. L. Smith; Mrs. J. Moye; Mrs. J. J. Pollard; and Mrs. W. M. Willis. My second endorsement of the resolution came less than a week later from the Pitt County chapter of the East Carolina Teachers College Alumni Association lead by Miss Ruth White and Mrs. Ruth Garner.

Meanwhile, Robert was moving across the state like a ball of fire, spreading the flame that was burning within him, speaking two or three times a day at civic clubs, book clubs, churches, and schools, booking as many speeches throughout the state and in adjoining states as he could possibly handle. In fact, a week or so later he telephoned me saying, "Jim, I am scheduled to speak to the Tarboro Rotary Club tomorrow night, but I am afraid my engagement in Richmond, Virginia, will make me late in arriving. Will you take Papa to the Rotary meeting in Tarboro, and if I am late, you take over?"

I had never seen a copy of Robert's speech on world federation because he always spoke extemporaneously, but I knew the basic ideas and I was able to recall the sequence of events. When Robert arrived at the Tarboro Rotary Club, I had been speaking ten to fifteen minutes. I could see him through the windows as he walked around the porch. When he entered the door, I greeted him in a low voice with these words, "I have just finished the Middle Ages." Without waiting to be introduced, Robert walked to the podium and began his speech with these words: "Just as the discovery of gunpowder in the thirteenth century signaled the end of the Middle Ages . . ." Immediately several Rotarians turned in their seats and stared at me. I had taken a front row seat considerably to the left of the podium and I could see them peripherally, but I continued to look at Robert. I must confess, however, that I was strongly tempted to drop my jaw, open wide my mouth, and raise my eyebrows as if to say: What a miracle!

During January most North Carolina legislators began to receive mail related to world federation. By the middle of February the pressure for action was beginning to be felt, and Robert decided that it was time for him to make a trip to Raleigh to speak with the legislators individually and to select a few leaders. By the first of March the General Assembly seemed ready to begin debate on the subject. Robert was then staying in and around Raleigh most of the time but continuing to make speeches in the area. I gave my last North Carolina speech on the subject in Durham near the end of the first week in March.

Perhaps one of the most interesting and devastating responses to an opponent of world federation during the debate in the North Carolina General Assembly came when a senator complained that the subject was so vast and its ramifications so numerous and complicated that he would need more time to study it. Whereupon a colleague responded, "I regret to have to inform the senator that civilization cannot wait for his intellectual development."

Since I had agreed to teach at Randolph Macon Academy the following year and also hoped to join the navy before the army drafted me, I did not continue the campaign with Robert into other states. Dr. Henry Leiper of Newark, New Jersey, persuaded Robert to take his campaign next to New Jersey.

With the backing of his home state he set out alone, quickly made acquaintances, and started his grassroots campaign across the state of New Jersey. After some months of campaigning, with many letters of endorsement being sent to legislators, he began to sense a light tone of opposition which seemed to follow him and repeat itself. After a few more weeks of hard campaigning, it became evident that the Hague machine had decided to oppose the resolution. Shortly thereafter, the resolution was brought before the legislature and quickly referred to a committee whose chairman was instructed to "bury it." The resolution was pigeonholed.

Apparently the leaders of the Hague machine were not apprised of the courage, stamina, and determination of Robert Lee Humber. On leaving the capitol in Trenton one day he smiled as he greeted a group of opposition leaders saying, "I hope you don't mind my returning to your constituents." They laughed replying, "No, go right ahead." He did just that, day after day, week after week, and month after month making sure always that letters kept pouring into Trenton. Finally, following an address one evening, a lady came to him and asked what the status of the resolution was at that time. When Robert explained that it had been sent to committee and pigeonholed, she was quite disappointed, but when he mentioned the name of the committee chairman her face brightened, and she broke into a broad smile saying, "May I have a copy of the resolution. He is a former student of mine. He is a good man, but I doubt if he has read the resolution." She spent the next day reading the resolution with the committee chairman. Within a week the resolution was brought out of committee and passed.

The voice of the people of New Jersey had finally been heard, and Robert Lee Humber had won his second state, but in terms of time consumed, it was a very costly win. North Carolina had required barely two and a half months to win. New Jersey had consumed more than a year of precious time.

Robert knew that he could not afford another New Jersey.

If he was going to persuade enough states to endorse the resolution and request their congressmen to support similar action in Congress in time to have any influence on the peace talks, he had to move faster. Thus he decided to start his grassroots campaign in several states simultaneously and also to make side trips into additional states whenever feasible. This he did, but the strain of two and sometimes three speeches a day plus constant travel began to take its toll. His voice became hoarse, and his doctor advised him to slow down because he might temporarily lose his voice and have to stop altogether.

A list of the states and the dates of their endorsement of the resolution reveal only in part the pressure under which he was working. When the campaign trail came to an end he had spoken a number of times in all the states on the continent between Canada and Mexico, and some of those states which are not listed below had passed the resolution in one house.

The resolution, with varying resolves, was adopted by the legislatures of:

North Carolina, March 13, 1941
New Jersey, May 1, 1942
Maryland, March 11, 1943
Connecticut, April 21, 1943
Rhode Island, April 22, 1943
Alabama, June 8, 1943
Virginia, March 8, 1944
Louisiana, July 5, 1944
Tennessee, February 27, 1945
Utah, March 2, 1945
Oklahoma, March 20, 1945
Florida, May 3, 1945
Georgia, January 31, 1946
Missouri, May 15, 1947
Kentucky, March 10, 1950

This was an astounding one-man achievement, but it was not the end of Robert Lee Humber's effort on behalf of world federation.

In 1945 he set up an appointment with Secretary of State Edward R. Stetinius for a meeting with representatives from twenty-two states which had shown great interest in world federation. Upon the death of President Roosevelt, however, this appointment was canceled.

Later, as a representative of the Southern Council of International Relations, Robert attended the San Francisco Conference at which the United Nations Charter was drafted.

Taking advantage of this excellent opportunity to learn what other nations were thinking about world federation, Robert interviewed the delegates of 80 percent of the nations represented. He was impressed with the intellectual depth and understanding of some of the delegates, and he was pleased to learn that most of the delegates he interviewed felt, as he did, that the United Nations Charter did not give the United Nations organization adequate power to accomplish its supreme assignment of eradicating war from this globe. He noted, however, that article 109 of the charter provides an opportunity to correct the weaknesses of the United Nations when it becomes obvious to its members and to world leaders that the United Nations cannot maintain world peace without at least the power to make, enforce, and adjudicate laws concerning the maintenance of peace. Its maximum power to make such laws would probably be limited to the minimum needed to assure peace.

Some years later Robert praised the humanitarian accomplishments of the United Nations organization and recommended continued support of the United Nations while it gained the experience and confidence necessary to seek the additional power it must have to maintain peace.

Chapter VII

While Robert was continuing his grassroots campaign across the United States, I was entering a new and unfamiliar world. Hoping to get in the navy in spite of my eye deficiency and the more rigid vision regulations which had just been announced, I took my letter of recommendation from former Secretary of the Navy Josephus Daniels and reported to the Naval Office in Norfolk, Virginia.

At the beginning of the eye examination I was told by one of the young examiners to stand with my toes touching the white line on the floor and read the chart. I read as far as I could and stopped. The examiners looked at one another; then one of them walked to the table where my "Dear Admiral" letter was lying and said, "Put your heels on the white line. Now read." As I squinted and tried to make out the next line on the chart, he added in a pleading tone of finality, "Lean forward." I did, but without success. The examiners graciously expressed their regrets that I could not meet the new, more stringent standards of the navy.

Upon reporting for duty at Fort Bragg, North Carolina, with a bus load of thirty-four-year-old draftees, I got the impression that the army was also adjusting its standards. The examiners were indeed perceptive. As we walked through the open doorway without bumping either side they apparently concluded that an eye examination would not be necessary. In fact, the only examination I recall their giving us at Fort Bragg was a group examination. I figured that the examiner, blessed with incredibly accurate vision and lightning-like eye movements, was probably a surveyor prior to entering the service. He marched twenty of us into a huge room and had us line up four feet apart. Then he ordered us to remove all our clothing and put it in a pile on the floor two feet in front of us. After sighting down the line again and getting it straight, he made a left face, took three steps forward, made a right face, and stood there a few seconds apparently getting a general perspective of the group. Then he marched parallel to our line, stopping for about six seconds in front of each man, making a quick survey of bare facts. Upon reaching the end of the line he ordered us to spread our legs, lean forward, and place our hands on our knees. Then he marched in the same manner behind us, stopping behind each man as if taking a back azimuth. Then while taking only six steps to the front of the room, with phenomenal speed and efficiency, he mentally computed the results and announced that we had all passed the examination and would be shipped out the following morning as "casuals" to Fort Slocum.

We were all anxious to do our part and win the war as rapidly as possible, but at Fort Slocum the mess sergeant, burdened at the end of our first day's work with more peeled potatoes than he could use in a week, informed us in no uncertain terms that we had the wrong idea. We took the sergeant's advice seriously and within less than two months we were given the privilege of an interview with an officer and shipped out.

My interview went as follows.

Lieutenant: "What were you in civilian life?"

Response: "A professor of French."

Lieutenant: "What in hell did you do? Never mind, you'll make a good ward boy."

Incidentally, before leaving Fort Slocum, I did get permission to go to Pelham Manor to hear Robert speak on world federation. He presented me to the audience which, to my pleasant surprise, included a Smith College graduate whom I had known in Paris during her junior year abroad. A small group of us used to sail together on the Seine below Paris, and I organized a ski trip for thirteen of us to a little village situated on the south side of a mountain high in the Alps near the Italian border, where we would have plenty of sunshine and still be assured of powdery snow during the Christmas holidays.

A few days after my interview, I was sent to Camp Shanks, where newly built, wooden, barrack-like wards facing a long ramp leading to the hospital were now ready for occupancy. After about three weeks of skillfully handling bedpans and accurately carrying them through the sensitive, sensory area of my superiors, I was promoted to corporal and stationed near the ward entrance, where it became my august duty to shout "Atten-hut" to announce the arrival of each doctor as he came to make his rounds.

Somehow, I always knew my voice lessons in Paris would pay off. I had a strong baritone, which resounded through the ward. Although I had no desire to disturb the peaceful atmosphere of the ward, I obeyed orders, and occasionally a sleeping patient, suddenly awakened, snapped to a sitting attention in his bed. Our ward was orderly, and I enjoyed being placed where I could see the daily activities and get some idea of the organization of the ward.

I also enjoyed watching the daily mealtime ramp parade put on by the carefree GU ward patients who, judging by the number of repeaters, would do most anything to avoid going overseas. The drill sergeant was a superb showman. He taught his smiling, slap-happy drill team to strut in a perfect, bouncy rhythm through intricate drill maneuvers. His last command of a series, usually given in front of the entrance to a ward, was actually the name by which this unique parade became known. The command was repeated quickly in order to force all the members of the drill team to turn in the opposite direction yet continue strutting in the original direction without missing a step, a bounce, or a beat. The quickly repeated command was "gonorrhea march."

I was gradually being introduced to new learning experiences, such as punching an orange with a hypodermic needle in order to develop a feeling for the pressure to apply when penetrating the skin. One day I was led into a small room to observe a young doctor make a spinal tap. A soldier was lying on his side on a table with his knees wrapped in his arms. As he began to pull his knees toward his body, thus curving his spine and opening what space there might be between the vertebrae, the young doctor began feeling along his spine with his fingertips, searching for the widest separation which might permit needle penetration; the senior doctor looked on and smiled his approval. Finally the young doctor found the spot where he believed the needle had the greatest possibility of penetrating without hitting an obstruction. He took the needle in hand, held it close to the soldier's skin, directly over the spot he had selected, then turned the needle slightly to get the angle he wanted and gave a quick jab. The soldier yelled in pain. The needle had not penetrated.

After some minutes to give the soldier time to settle down

and relax, the same procedure began again. The young doctor found a new location between two other vertebrae and there he made a second quick jab. Again the soldier yelled in pain and again the needle failed to penetrate. The time between the second and third attempts was long enough for me to reflect on the situation. I appreciated the senior doctor's wanting me to observe the spinal tap, and if there was anything I could do to help anyone, I wanted to remain; but I knew that my presence wasn't helping anyone in that room. I nodded to the senior doctor and quietly withdrew. I do not know how the third try came out. I never asked.

A month or so later with a few more chores added to my duties, I was given the rank of sergeant, but I was not happy. My age had caused me to be classified "permanent party in America" and because a second lieutenant didn't know what to do with a professor of French, I had been placed in medics, a field in which I had absolutely no background.

With a good background in French, I felt almost as if I were betraying my country and France by not going overseas and trying to serve in a way that most Americans would not be able to serve. I held a master's degree in French from Harvard University, a *Diplôme superieur d'études françaises modernes* from the Alliance Française of Paris, a diplôme from the Institut de Phonétiques of the Université de Paris, and was working toward the *Doctorat de l'Université de Paris* when war broke out. I had spent a number of years of my life in France studying the French people, their language, their literature, and their country, most of which I had covered by bicycle, automobile, or train. Furthermore, I didn't leave France when war was declared; I stayed until Marshal Pétain laid down arms on June 25, 1940. In other words, my firsthand knowledge of France, however limited, was as up-to-date as that of any American, other than possibly a spy who had been left behind or placed in the country after Hitler took over.

Perhaps it was my observation of the young doctor's effort to make a spinal tap which reminded me that the level of service anyone can render in any field is limited to his level of education and experience in that field. In any case I did not want to waste any more time. I put in a request to be transferred to the first outfit on alert to go overseas. My request was denied because I had never been given basic training. I then requested that I be given basic training. When it was discovered that five other soldiers in our outfit were making similar requests for overseas service, and being denied for the same reason, a sergeant was assigned the task of giving us basic training.

The first day of basic training we were given a lesson in cover and concealment. Dressed in fatigues, we were taken to the edge of a woods, handed some small paper bags stuffed with white flour, and told to put them in our pockets. They were our ammunition which would leave evidence on our clothing when we were knocked out of combat. Then three of us (the Indians) were instructed to hide in the woods. After a few minutes the other three (the cowboys) were sent in to destroy the enemy.

The next day we were taken to an infiltration course where we crawled on our stomachs on rugged ground toward a machine gun firing tracer bullets over our heads. When we came to barbed wire, we rolled over on our backs and passed beneath the wire. A major, whose chest and belly merged to form a crescent from his neck to the seat of his pants, got down on the ground to show us how it was done. I knew I could crawl as fast as he could, so I got down beside him. That was a big mistake. The sergeant in charge of firing the dynamite charges planted along the way fired only when the major was nearby. The earth rose a foot or so and fell heavily on the major and me. When we finished the course the major and I were covered with dirt from head to foot. Thus ended my basic training.

The next day I was taken to Camp Kilmer and transferred to the transportation corps, which was on alert. Early the following morning, I tried to do bayonet practice, which I had never before even witnessed. After another day of subconsciously avoiding all second lieutenants for fear I would become a grease monkey in some motor pool, I was shipped out.

I had crossed the Atlantic on four different transatlantic steamers, but this was by far the largest, fastest, and most queenly floating casino I had ever seen. I had visited the casino at Monte Carlo when I was twenty-one years old, but I didn't gamble because my freshman year in college had taught me better. I had registered late for school and was forced to take a room on the third floor in a downtown building over a drugstore and a hardware store at a time when freshmen either ran errands for upperclassmen or suffered rather unpleasant consequences. My knowledge of card games, limited to Rook and Flinch, suddenly expanded to include numerous variations of poker, gin, and blackjack, and my acquaintance with gambling even extended to a fair knowledge of roulette. Yes, the roulette wheel and the felt table cover were in a room on the third floor, but they were not used very often. The card game, however, ran almost continuously, night and day. The players, knowing that I would keep a poker face, often turned up the corner of their hole card, when playing stud, to show me the basis for their betting. Of course it also told me who would bluff and who would not.

The great *Ocean Queen* was so packed with soldiers that its beautiful interior could hardly be seen, but the mass of gambling humanity was a sight to behold. There were the grinning winners anxious to keep the game moving as fast as possible. Some, following an old habit, kept getting up and leaving the game temporarily to stash away some of their winnings to keep others from knowing how much they were winning. And of course there were plenty of the other extreme, the losers and their pathetic colleagues, so typical of that card room habitué who always gets a strong feeling that a winning streak is due and wants to borrow just enough money to get started again.

This great floating casino, however, was not typical of the average casino. The men on board, from general to private, knew that they had only a few days to take advantage of an incredible opportunity. The stakes were high and the gambling fast and furious. It seemed that every player was determined to make a million or go broke. Even on deck, wherever the wind was not blowing too hard, the crap shooters sitting on army blankets crowded out most of the walking space.

This incredible voyage across the north Atlantic must now be relegated to the unreal world of fantasy. An incredible set of circumstances converged to assemble in one place, at a given moment, thousands of men from across the North American continent and crowd them into the world's largest and fastest super ocean liner, keeping them huddled together for more than four days while traveling at high speed through dangerous submarine-infested waters toward a frightfully dangerous and even questionable future. It would be difficult indeed to imagine a set of circumstances more conducive to complete abandon to a gambling orgy and I doubt that one of this magnitude will ever again occur. It was an unreal event belonging only to this one short period of time in the history of man.

Although I did not roll the dice or play cards, I had a thrilling but deceivingly short voyage to Scotland. It was made more pleasant and also more unreal to me when a second lieutenant who spotted me in the lounge came to ask me where I would prefer to be stationed in England. Skeptically, I listed three choices: Oxford, Cambridge, and London, and, to my amazement, I was sent to the delightful university town of Cambridge, which I thoroughly enjoyed. Upon arrival at Cambridge, I was made to feel at home in my new environment when my commanding officer, who had read my file, told me that he was reserving two hours three afternoons a week for me to teach French to those members of his outfit who might want to pick up a little French. I was delighted that at last I would be able to render some service in a field with which I was familiar. The only GI material available on the subject at the time was the Linguaphone set of recordings and the accompanying texts, which were definitely not designed for army use. They could be used nevertheless for listening and reading practice. With a practical conversational approach in mind, I drew up a series of short lesson plans which could be adjusted to the background and ability of the men. I also counted on spending considerable time in each class answering questions in French about France, its geography, its highway and railway organization, its people, etc. I knew, of course, that I would have to follow up with some translation for those who did not understand spoken French.

After I had been in Cambridge a few months and had sampled a little of most of the activities around the university except "punting on the Cam," my commanding officer informed me that he had received a request from the university asking if I would substitute the following day for Professor Frank Doby, an American exchange professor from Texas, who would be out of town for the day and needed someone to take over his class of cadets. I knew that Professor Doby had the reputation of being an interesting teacher who was very proud of the great state of Texas, and I could tell that my commanding officer wanted me to accept the "invitation," so I did.

The next morning when I walked into the classroom, even before introducing myself, I turned to the blackboard and drew an outline sketch of the eastern coastline of the United

States. As I reached North Carolina, I made the state considerably larger than normal, and when I reached the gulf coastline of Texas, I made that state appear much smaller than normal. Before I could put down the chalk and turn around, the cadets were laughing and I knew I had a good audience.

I told them that I had no desire to belittle the state of Texas, but I wanted to tell them about recent events taking place in North Carolina which could give our struggle in this war a greater purpose than merely that of ending the careers of ambitious dictators. I then gave them a condensed story of the background and work of my friend and neighbor Robert Lee Humber of Greenville, North Carolina, who at twelve years of age decided that he wanted to become a Rhodes scholar. I mentioned his education at Wake Forest College where he received his A.B. and L.L.B. degrees; his short period of military service in France near the close of World War I; his return to Harvard University for his M.A.; his being named Rhodes scholar from the state of North Carolina to Oxford, where he received the degree of bachelor of English literature; his years of study in Paris working toward the Doctorat de l'état, the highest degree that France offers; his decision to interrupt his studies in order to get married and to accept the directorship of the European headquarters of an American oil firm, whose offices were located on the Champs Elysées in Paris.

I then mentioned that, in the meantime, I had returned to Paris to continue my studies, and we were both there when the war broke out. We left France June 25, 1940, the day that Marshal Pétain laid down arms, and returned to Greenville, North Carolina. Within three months after our return Mr. Humber completed the writing of the Declaration of the Federation of the World—a document which embodied the conclusions he had reached after years of study and research concerning the steps necessary to be taken in order to establish and maintain peace on this globe.

With that document in hand, he started a grassroots campaign across the state of North Carolina. Within two and a half months the North Carolina General Assembly endorsed the document in the form of a Legislative resolution on March 13, 1941. Copies were sent to North Carolina's congressmen in Washington, D.C. Since that time, Mr. Humber had gotten endorsements from the legislators of New Jersey, Maryland,

Connecticut, Rhode Island and Alabama, and he is continuing his campaign, I told them, into other states as rapidly as possible. If he can get enough endorsements before the end of this war, I said, he could have some influence on the peace talks that follow, and at last we might find ourselves in a position to try to fulfill the prophesies which Tennyson expressed in the last verse of *Locksley Hall:*

> *Til the war-drum throbb'd no longer and the*
> *battle flags were furl'd*
> *In the Parliament of man, the Federation of*
> *the world.*

In my closing remarks to the cadets, I quoted, as well as I could remember, the following excerpt from Mr. Humber's declaration:

History has revealed but one principle by which free peoples, inhabiting extensive territories, can unite under one government without impairing their local autonomy. That principle is federation, whose virtue preserves the whole without destroying its parts and strengthens its parts without jeopardizing the whole. Federation vitalizes all nations by endowing them with security and freedom to develop their respective cultures without menace of foreign domination. It regards as sacrosanct man's personality, his rights as an individual and as a citizen and his role as a partner with all other men in the common enterprise of building civilization for the benefit of mankind. It suppresses the crime of war by reducing to the ultimate minimum the possibility of its occurrence. It renders unnecessary the further paralyzing expenditure of wealth for belligerent activity, and cancels through the ages the mortgages of war against the fortunes and services of men. It releases the full energies, intelligence and assets of society for creative, ameliorative and redemptive work on behalf of humanity. It apprehends the entire human race as one family, human beings everywhere as brothers and all nations as component parts of an indivisible community.

The applause that followed these remarks was truly rewarding. I felt that I had succeeded in striking a spark of optimism and hope at a time when it was sorely needed by all of us and so thoroughly deserved by the British, who had borne the heaviest burden for so long a time. The cadets became highly interested in world federation and continued to discuss it long after leaving the halls of the university. A week later I received news of their discussions from numerous sources, including indirectly from Professor Doby.

Then one day my commanding officer called me into his office to tell me that a British colonel had asked if I would join a brain trust under his command, which he was planning to take to a number of troop concentrations in East Anglia. I deferred to my commander, who encouraged me to accept the invitation. A brain trust, I learned, was what most Americans would call a panel discussion group. Each member of the panel gave a short talk, then the members of the audience fired questions at the panel. I accepted the invitation because I wanted to keep alive the idea of world federation, which was then, and, incidentally, still is to me, the best idea yet presented which can and some day may lead to a lasting world peace.

Over a period of several weeks we made a number of appearances before troop concentrations in East Anglia. The sincerity of my conviction concerning the necessity of world law drew excellent questions, enabling me to develop the thesis of world federation. At the same time, my status as the only non-com on the panel permitted me to enjoy the sympathetic bias of the soldiers and add a bit of levity to our performance. I couldn't have asked for a better situation.

After our last brain trust appearance the colonel added our names to the guest list for a dinner party he was giving to a number of officers stationed at Cambridge. I was seated next to a Russian officer by the name of Kovarski. He reminded me of a big, relaxed midwesterner, thoroughly self-confident and absolutely frank and easy to talk to. I couldn't resist the temptation to ask him about Russian relations with the Baltic countries. His simple response was that they were Russian before, they would be Russian again. Later, after the atomic bomb was dropped, I wondered if Kovarski was one of the physicists stationed at Cambridge during the war.

Chapter VIII

Shortly after my brain trust experience, my commanding officer called me to his office and asked if I would like to be recommended for officer's training. I said I would. He told me to have a seat while he called headquarters. Apparently informed that they were no longer taking applications, he asked, "What about a direct commission?" Then after a brief discussion, he put down the receiver, turned to me, and said, "I was told, 'If he is that good, send him to headquarters.'"

When I reported to the advanced section of the transportation corps headquarters in London, it appeared that some reorganization was taking place. No one knew who had asked that I be sent to London. One lieutenant said that he could use me. Thus I became a messenger boy. From a ward boy in America, to a very pleasant interlude in Cambridge, to beginning all over again in a new outfit as a messenger boy in London, I thought *plus ça change plus c'est la même chose.*

After carrying messages for a week, I became bored and applied for permission to join the Churchill Club, which met at regular intervals in a large room in Westminster Abbey for tea and programs, mostly lectures. I enjoyed the programs I attended and was highly amused and almost embarrassed on one occasion by the behavior of a group of American doctors, who at that time were so bitterly opposed to the idea of socialized medicine that they reacted to the address by a member of the Canadian Parliament like frustrated little boys afraid someone was going to steal their marbles.

London at that time was not the safest place to be. The great devastating blitz had come to an end, but for psychological reasons and to keep the regular pattern of life off balance, the Nazis continued to strike London almost every day and night with their "buzz bombs." When the first ones came in we knew that they would head straight to earth when the motor cut off. Later they set the rudders so the bombs would circle before hitting the ground. Then they added a screaming whistle to the descent. One night a bomb hit so close by that I was jolted out of the top bunk of a double-deck bed. Another night I went to a first-class restaurant to get a change from army food. As I was eating my dessert, the air-raid alarm sounded. I finished my meal and entered an air raid shelter next door in a basement two floors below street level. Someone started a recording of Bach's "Air for a G String" and I drifted off with the beautiful music, completely oblivious to the raid. When the music ended, I had to ask if the "all clear" had sounded.

One day at advanced headquarters I was handed an aerial photograph to deliver to the intelligence office. I looked at the photograph, and when I handed it to the officer in charge, I said, "Major, this is a photograph of the PLM tracks a few miles southeast of Paris near Villeneuve Triage. About one half mile north of where this bomb hit, two tracks cross over two other tracks. At that point, unless the pilot was instructed to cut only these two tracks, he could have made four tracks unusable with that one bomb." The next morning, I was transferred to the intelligence branch of the advanced section of our headquarters, where I remained until after VJ Day.

About a week later, after being issued a new tommy gun, firing it one burst, then spending the rest of the day taking it apart and putting it back together, we headed across the channel to Normandy. As we approached the French coast, I was asked if I could drive a jeep. After delivering an affirmative reply, I was ordered over the side of the transport and down a network of ropes into a small landing craft loaded with jeeps. I threw my equipment in the third jeep from the front of a line, and when the landing craft stopped, drove ashore following the two jeeps ahead of me into the dunes. We camped in an area north of Saint Lo a few days until after the breakthrough occurred. Then during the early morning hours before daylight, I was awakened and told to bring my equipment. It had been raining during the night, so I gave my mattress cover stuffed with hay which I had gotten from a French farmer to the soldier next to me to get him out of the mud. I then carried the rest of my equipment to the jeep. When I arrived, two colonels were waiting. One, a West Point graduate, had already placed himself in the middle of the back seat between his equipment roll on one side and that of the other colonel on the other side. As I approached, I asked him if he would mind loading my tommy gun while I adjusted my equipment roll, as it was coming apart. "Don't you know how to load it?" he asked excitedly. "Yes," I replied, "I'm just trying to save us some time." "Hand me your roll," he said, "and you load your gun." He took my equipment roll and stuffed it behind him for additional protection, and it dawned on me that he probably had never seen the new tommy gun and didn't know how to load it.

The other colonel, considerably older, was obviously not of the military. I figured that he was probably a top-notch railroad man, whom they had given the rank of colonel in order to have his "know-how" close by at all times. The first thing I told him when we started out was that I doubted that I would be able to drive and use that mulish tommy gun at the same time. In case of trouble, therefore, I would suggest that he hold on tightly and I would probably step on the gas and possibly zigzag a little. The only disturbance I anticipated was the possibility of some German troops rushing out to surrender to us rather than to the people whose country they had occupied for the past four years.

The mission of which we were a part was to go west along the coast in search of a good, usable harbor. On our first lap to Dinard, I was the only person hit by a projectile. One of a group of French farm workers gathering onions recognized us as Americans and tossed an onion which I was unable to catch while steering the jeep. It hit me on my helmet. I told my backseat colonel that I was going to put in for the Purple Heart, but I don't believe he thought it was very funny. After all, if the onion had missed me, it could have hit him.

We were among the first to arrive at Dinard, a little town which I had visited once before when I was a student in France. At the hotel desk, I requested two rooms, a double and a single. The desk clerk, who I think was also the owner of the establishment, led the two colonels to the double room and came back to show me to my room. Although he seemed to understand English, I could tell that he appreciated meeting foreigners who could speak his language. I told him if he had any problem understanding any of our group and wanted to call on me, I would be glad to help. During the night I was awakened by the loud voice of an angry man shouting, "I don't want to sleep there. I want a room. " I could not clearly

81

hear what the clerk was saying, but it sounded as if he was assuring the man that the hay was fresh and clean.

The next day we continued to the fishing village of Roscoff. I was not told anything about the success or failure of our mission, but the delicious lobster dinner we were served that night and the spotlessly clean and comfortable bed I slept in was success to me. As we left the inn the following morning and approached our vehicles to leave, someone behind me said, "Tell them we have to leave now to pursue the enemy into Germany." I did, and to my "jusqu'en Allemagne" a French lady added "jusqu'à Berlin." I agreed with her and then expressed our thanks for their gracious hospitality, ending my remarks with "vive la France. " Everybody joined in. A Frenchman added "vive l'FFI" (Forces Françaises de l'- Interieur or the French underground forces), in which we joined.

Soon after our headquarters were established in Paris, I was sent to a meeting in which the British, French and Americans were all pressing their claim to the full use of the few remaining refrigerated railway cars in France. The French, of course, claimed the cars because they needed to supply their troops and their people, who had been deprived of a proper diet for the past four years. Both the British and Americans, however, insisted that they had to have the cars to supply their troops. The more they argued, the more frustrated they became, and the more frustrated they became, the more a few of them began to lose their composure. For awhile during the heat of the argument when an interpreter was called on, it was no longer "tell the gentleman" but "tell that so and so." That did not last, however, because when they reached that point, they had also reached an impasse, which some of them had probably anticipated from the start. Now that they had all established their determination to fight for what they wanted, they could work out a compromise.

Strategy of that type sometimes gets good results, but it's tough on interpreters, who always feel the need to keep emotions on an even keel. I often wondered how Herr Schmidt, Hitler's interpreter, handled that problem. The first time I heard Herr Schmidt, I was at a student conference which my sister Louise and I attended in Vienna in 1928. He was translating at that time for Chancellor Kurt von Schuschnigg and doing a beautiful job, but translating for Hitler, who imprisoned Schuschnigg! I wondered how Herr Schmidt could stomach working for Hitler.

As American GI's began to pour into Paris, I decided I had better purchase some gifts to send home before the store shelves were depleted. I went to a perfume shop and told the saleslady that I wanted several bottles of perfume. She asked, "Is it for a blond or a brunette, a young person or an elderly person, the delicate or athletic type, for morning wear or evening wear?" At that point I interrupted saying, "Madame, when I go to a restaurant and order a certain cut of meat or a certain kind of cheese and I want wine to go with it, I have learned that I get better results when I ask the waiter to select the wine he thinks goes best with it. Now, I am not a connoisseur of wines or perfumes, and I have no ambition to become a "nez," but I have a very keen, though relatively uneducated, sense of smell. If you will prove to me that there is a definite relationship between certain scents and certain types of individuals, I will trust your judgment in selecting a number of quality gifts for me." She replied, "OK, I'll let you prove it to yourself."

She went behind the counter, pulled two pages from a small notepad, and wrote something on each sheet. Then she folded one sheet and placed it in a small cloth sack, put a bottle of perfume in the same sack, and pulled a drawstring around the neck of the bottle so the name of the perfume could not be seen. Then she did the same with the second piece of paper and a second bottle of perfume. "Now," she said, "take a light sniff of this perfume and describe the lady to me." I sniffed and immediately replied, "She is definitely a blond." "Anything else?" she asked. "Well, she is light and airy." The saleslady opened the sack, unfolded the paper and handed it to me. I read in her handwriting, "Quelques fleurs—Houbigant—une blonde délicate." Then, following the same procedure, I got from the second scent the image of a heavy brunette and I read the accompanying paper. "Tabu—Jean Patou—une brune athlétique."

I knew that the saleslady had given me the simplest test possible, but she had proved her point, and I sent ten bottles of perfume home for my mother to give to her friends at Christmastime. Later, I learned that my mother had invited five of her friends to come by the house and choose the bottles they wanted. Then she and my two sisters took one bottle each and sent the remaining two to friends in Wilson, North Carolina. After the war, I stopped by to see one of my mother's Wilson friends. She greeted me with a big hug and thanked me for that wonderful "Moment Supreme."

One day as the courier was leaving the general's office, he passed my desk and told me that he was headed for Epernay. I said, "How about bringing me a case of champagne?" Two days later he placed the case of champagne on top of my filing cabinet. While I was settling up with him and thanking him, I told him that I was going to surprise a cousin of mine in Greenville, North Carolina, who holds open house for his friends every year at Christmas. That's when I learned that military regulations would not permit me to send the champagne to America. I took the bottles out of the case and placed them in the lower drawers of my filing cabinet, where I kept them until Christmas. We shared two or three bottles in the office, and I gave the others to individual staff members. Though I am not a *dégustateur*, I think it was the best champagne I have ever tasted. It was very light and effervescent, and I don't think I ever told cousin Charlie that he missed a case of Pommery et Greyno's "Drapeau Sec" which I think the courier went all the way to Reims to get.

In the middle of December, with a terrible cold and a fever of 103 degrees, I was sent to the American Hospital in Paris. I had been there only three days, when, all of a sudden, in the middle of the night I was awakened and told to put on my clothes and gather my things. I was then rushed down to a waiting military vehicle, a blanket was thrown around me, and with a few other patients, I was driven twenty or more miles, where I was directed to a bed in a huge, unheated dormitory containing long lines of empty beds. I did not know where I was, but I knew that there was serious trouble somewhere along the front, and I figured that the American Hospital in Paris was probably being reserved for surgical cases only. I took off only my shoes and got in bed with my uniform and my overcoat still on. Someone threw a blanket over me, and as I pulled it up around my neck, I knocked a clod of dry mud off the blanket onto the floor. I slept warmly, comfortably, and soundly, but I was awakened early in the morning by a dreadful cacophony of war sounds coming from the strained throats of battle-weary soldiers.

The huge room had been filled during the night. The eyes of some stared but seemed not to see anything. One soldier was standing in the middle of his bed, his arms stretched out like the wings of a plane. To the vocal roar of a motor and the ack-ack of machine guns, he was twisting and turning and diving and firing at the enemy. Another, whose face revealed that he had no idea what he was doing, was doing a perfect imitation of Woody Woodpecker.

Sitting on the side of a bed not far from me, a strong, healthy looking man was talking and crying at the same time. He was a tank commander whose younger brother, Joey, had always idolized him. Joey had volunteered for military service as soon as he was old enough so he could fight beside his brother. At last he had gotten into the same tank division with his big brother, who was now sitting there on the side of the bed crying like a baby, saying that he was sure they would kill Joey, who was too young and inexperienced to know how to protect himself.

A few days later at headquarters in Paris, I read the daily newspaper account of the Battle of the Bulge, and I thought about Joey and his big brother. Tears ran down my cheeks, and I found it very difficult not to cry like a baby, too.

In the spring following the Battle of the Bulge, it seemed that the Nazis were being pushed back or falling back on all fronts, and I was beginning to anticipate the end of the war. I had been advanced to the rank of staff sergeant, a promotion I hadn't expected because the major who was apparently responsible for having me placed in the intelligence office had left that office soon after we arrived in Paris. In any case, I was grateful to the person who recommended me for promotion, whoever he was.

On May 8, VE Day, I knew it was time for me to do some postwar planning and naturally my thoughts turned first to Greenville and East Carolina Teachers College. I wrote home and learned that Mr. Ralph Deal, professor of French and chairman of the Department of Foreign Languages at East Carolina Teachers College, was planning to retire. I therefore sent my credentials and applied for the position.

When I was offered Mr. Deal's position in July, I hastened to the French Ministry of Information and asked if they had any realia, or in today's lingo, visual aids, which they could make available to me in my new position. They asked for suggestions, and I modestly mentioned posters, maps, and pictures. They replied that they would be happy to send those items plus some others which they thought would be useful to me.

I thanked them, then went on a shopping spree, seeking

French objects which I thought would interest my students. I found a beautiful scarf commemorating the four battles of the liberation of Paris, a disque recorded by the FFI (French underground forces) of the battle which took place in front of Notre Dame, and an attractive pair of ladies' wooden slippers made for the stylish Parisienne during the occupation years when leather was no longer available.

In the afternoon I was hunting in the bookstalls along the Seine near Boulevard Saint Michel for Nazi propaganda leaflets, when Raymond Duncan and his companion stopped to browse. Calling him by name, I introduced myself. After a brief conversation, he invited me to have tea with them at the nearby Academia Raymond Duncan. His companion, a gracious woman whose name I can no longer recall, prepared a pot of tea and joined us. I told them of the teaching position I had just accepted and of my search for souvenirs of Paris which might interest my students. He told me of his activities during the occupation and showed me the wooden alphabet set which he had carved and used to print the news sheet he distributed at regular intervals He used his news sheet to announce the musicals and numerous other gatherings held at the Academia Raymond Duncan. I wanted to ask him for a souvenir of the academia to take back with me, because I felt certain that some of my students would have heard of him and his sister Isadora. But I didn't, because I knew that he had made almost everything there with his own hands, even the tunic and sandals he was wearing.

When VJ Day came on August 14, I held in my hands evidence that I had accepted the position of chairman of the Department of Foreign Languages and professor of French at East Carolina Teachers College in Greenville, North Carolina, and was expected to report to work at the beginning of the fall quarter. With that evidence in hand I was able to request early transportation back to America. I was told that, in fact, I would probably be returned by air.

It turned out to be the rather indelicate air of hundreds of men packed like sardines in the lower bowels of a liberty ship. In spite of the crowded conditions, we were happy to return on any ship under any circumstances. When we stepped off that ship onto American soil and took in a deep breath of fresh air, all of us, black and white, felt emancipated at last.

Chapter IX

Upon my arrival in Greenville, North Carolina, I was eager to see the latest East Carolina Teachers College catalogue and to talk with Professor Ralph Deal, the retiring chairman of the Department of Foreign Languages. I had learned in conversation with him during a beach trip in the 1930s that President Robert H. Wright had "given him permission" to plan a foreign language curriculum in 1921, the year that East Carolina Teachers Training School became East Carolina Teachers College. Professor Deal's program, consisting of fifteen French courses and fifteen Latin courses, did not make its appearance, however, until the time of the 1923-24 catalogue.

By 1945, when I arrived on campus, Latin had disappeared from high school offerings and the Latin courses at East Carolina Teachers College had given way to a modern foreign language program consisting of thirty-two French courses, eighteen Spanish courses, and six German courses for a total of 130 quarter hours. This was an ambitious program, which I knew would overload the schedules of a chairman and one teacher, and I wondered why Professor Deal had not added another teacher to the department.

To seek an answer to this and other questions which came to mind, I turned to the first page of the 1944-45 E.C.T.C. catalogue and started reading. When I reached page 41, I found under the heading of "Admissions from High School," a one-sentence paragraph announcing: "A foreign language is not required for admission."

To a biased French teacher, just arriving to take over chairmanship of the Department of Foreign Languages, this statement looked more like a neon sign flashing, "Come one, come all to EZTC." I was astounded at the catalogue statement because, at that time, most colleges and universities were re-

87

quiring two years of one foreign language for admission. If the student could not meet the requirement, he was admitted with a deficiency, which he could remove by the end of his sophomore year. I was also keenly aware that freshmen were regularly advised to remove required courses first. Thus, the lack of a foreign language entrance requirement denied the Department of Foreign Languages the privilege of meeting potential foreign language majors their freshman year, and this, in turn, made it extremely difficult, if not impossible, to build a strong four-year foreign language program.

After reading a few more pages in the catalogue, I learned that E.C.T.C. was offering three degrees, the A.B., B.S. and M.A., but no foreign language was required for graduation with any of these degrees. With no foreign language entrance requirement and no foreign language graduation requirement, it was not surprising to me that Professor Deal had too few foreign language students in his department to justify an additional foreign language teacher. I did not fault Professor Deal, who was an intelligent person. On the contrary, I marveled at his ingenuity in keeping, under the circumstances, the Department of Foreign Languages alive for twenty-two years.

I knew also that President Wright had set up his teacher training program in the framework of the A.B. degree and originally used Latin to give it the depth he felt it needed. Meanwhile, however, most high schools had replaced Latin by French, the modern foreign language credited with having furnished more than half the words of the English language. Colleges and universities encouraged this trend by adding approximately two years of one modern foreign language to their admissions requirements. I found, however, that the transition to a strong liberal arts degree at East Carolina Teachers College had not taken place. Neither Latin nor a modern foreign language had become an integral part of the liberal arts program.

Although I had no desire to force the study of a foreign language on students who didn't want it, I felt it my duty to correct the weakness of our liberal arts degree. I also knew that a foreign language departmental chairman who had just arrived on campus would make a grave mistake if he tried to force the issue. I was aware that the change would require time and patience and might even have to be accomplished through others, who would be less directly affected by the change.

I was nonetheless convinced that man sharpens his knowledge of all things by means of comparison, and I saw little in the curriculum of E.C.T.C. with which the student could compare the English language or American civilization. As a native of Greenville, I was fully aware that prior to the two world wars, few people in eastern North Carolina had enjoyed the opportunity of observing their own country and its civilization through foreign eyes. Most people were relatively limited in their ability to see their country objectively and to comprehend the leadership role among nations which their wealth and power were forcing upon their nation and ultimately on them, as responsible citizens of the world.

I remembered vividly getting my first truly objective glimpse of my country when I finally penetrated the veil of a foreign language and began to understand and appreciate a great foreign nation, whose constitution states that it "is a republic, indivisible, secular, democratic, and social," whose motto is "Liberty, Equality, Fraternity," and whose principle is "government of the people, for the people, by the people." Here was a democracy which permitted and even seemed to encourage the election of both royalists and communists to its Chambre des Députés (House of Representatives).

In my studies abroad at that time, I came upon old newspaper accounts of Woodrow Wilson's proposal of a League of Nations to establish and maintain world peace. When the U.S. Senate, primarily because of internal political jealousies, failed to ratify the League, European newspaper headlines screamed in horror: "America Abandons Her Own Beautiful Child." Gradually, I began to understand the European feeling that the United States of America is like a Big American Boy, always ready to do his share but not yet mature enough to set priorities which would permit him to place the peace of all mankind ahead of his own internal political squabbles.

Now, at East Carolina Teachers College in 1945, I was concerned that this Big American Boy would have little opportunity of ever reaching the level of maturity expected of him unless the educational institutions of his nation provided a truly broad basic education, one unafraid to challenge any theory in any field of learning. Only then would he be capable of sharpening his intellect and broadening his knowledge, finally enabling him to remove at least his share of that great international barrier of ignorance, superstition, and prejudice which still separates men and nations on this globe. I was, therefore, anxious to encourage the addition to the E.C.T.C. curriculum of those features which would lead to an understanding of the interrelationship of men and nations throughout the world and lay the foundation for enlightened opinion, which, I believed, should characterize every intelligent citizen. I wanted our institution to challenge, inspire, and prepare the youth of today for the leadership of tomorrow. I wanted the best for E.C.T.C. and I knew that a liberal arts program which did not include the study of a foreign language and its civilization was not the best.

When Miss Marguerite Austin and I started the school year with no professional secretarial assistance and only one student helper—who had to divide her time among three departments (the Geography Department, the Industrial Arts Department, and the Department of Foreign Languages)—I understood that I would have to face time-consuming chores which I had not anticipated. Immediately, I made plans to register for a course in touch-typing as soon as I could, and I put aside all thoughts of making alterations in departmental offerings and the catalogue until a later date. That year, we simply concentrated on the preparation and teaching of the foreign language courses scheduled. To the two of us, who loved our work, that was great fun. I even felt free enough to accept membership in the Greenville Rotary Club, and the following year, I sponsored Robert Lee Humber for membership in Rotary.

When the boxes of realia from the French government arrived, I was astounded to see such a quantity of quality gifts, including a number of beautiful Duffy posters and more than one hundred large glossy photographs, depicting everything from the leading allied officers of the war to the latest French styles for the ladies. Included were numerous copies of magazines and books published during the war years and a handsome leather-bound loose-leaf atlas, containing some of the most beautifully colored map studies I have ever seen. Each map was a thorough scientific study and a work of art.

These artistic and literary French creations of the war years, plus others which I had purchased and brought back with me, inspired our first effort to introduce the postwar Department of Foreign Languages and its "new deal" to the campus of East Carolina Teachers College. Marguerite and I devoted long hours to the planning and preparing of an exhibit, which we entitled "France 1939-45." The exhibit turned out to be so large that we had to seek space for its presentation in the nearby Flanagan Building, to which the two of us transported all the realia. We arranged everything to tell a vivid story of the beautiful but struggling French nation from the time of the declaration of war, September 3, 1939, to VE Day, May 8, 1945.

The exhibit material was so timely that we were convinced no other college or university in America could mount anything comparable to it at that time, and of course we hoped for a large attendance. As it turned out, however, Marguerite and I decided that we preferred to judge the success of our exhibit not by the number of persons attending, but by the apparent enthusiasm of those who did come.

The first persons to arrive at the exhibit were Howard J. McGinnis, president of E.C.T.C., and Mr. Herbert Waldrop, a member of the E.C.T.C. Board of Trustees. They were followed by Mr. F. D. Duncan and other administrative officers. The faculty members and townspeople seemed to arrive in little groups which could be categorized as Marguerite's friends, my friends, and my mother's friends. The students who came were members of our classes and their friends.

Since I was in France when war was declared and did not leave until Marshal Pétain laid down arms June 25, 1940, I was able to serve as a guide through the exhibit, giving each group of visitors the noteworthy details of each item on exhibit and a blow-by-blow account of what was happening in France at the time.

The exhibit tour terminated at a large "peace" table, on which was centered a globe of the world. Lying on the table at the foot of the globe was a pamphlet entitled "The Declaration of the Federation of the World" written by Robert Lee Humber in the fall of 1940 and a colorful silk scarf commemorating the four battles of the Liberation of Paris, which took place during the week of August 19-26, 1944.

When I returned to Paris as an American soldier in 1944 and purchased the scarf commemorating the Liberation of Paris, I was reminded of the beautiful concert given in the winter of 1940 to our students Atelier in Paris by the talented concert team of the attractive pianist Nadia Tagrine and her young violinist brother. In August of 1944 he was killed while fighting for the liberation of Paris, and Nadia was devastated at the loss of her brother and concert partner. The scarf has since been framed and hangs above the mantelpiece in my den. I plan to give it to East Carolina University to be placed in the seminar room which the university so graciously dedicated to me when I retired in 1970.

The great influx of servicemen returning from overseas helped to change the attitude of East Carolina Teachers College students toward the study of foreign languages. In the summer of 1948, Miss Austin and I offered an accelerated beginning French course designed to help those students who had not been required to take a foreign language at East Carolina Teachers College, but who were planning to continue their studies at graduate schools where a reading knowledge of one foreign language was required. We crowded into one session of summer school (six weeks) all the material that would normally be covered in a beginning language course lasting one full year. The students had to attend five hours of French classes per day, plus do laboratory work in the afternoon to prepare for recitation the following day. Marguerite and I alternated as teachers of the course. I took the eight o'clock hour, Marguerite the nine, and so on. It was a strenuous six weeks in which Marguerite and I became so involved that we occasionally visited one another's teaching hour. A few days after the end of the course, we were pleasantly surprised to read the following article, which appeared in the student newspaper:

Yankee-Rebel French Class Taught
Year's French Work In Six Weeks

The TECO ECHO
Greenville, N.C., Friday, July 30, 1948
Summer Edition, No. 4
by Richard Tarravechia

So you want to learn a year of French in six weeks? Well, step right up, mes amis, walk casually up to room 206 in the Austin building, and put in your reservation for a strait-jacket. Oh yes, they're standard equipment for the course.

You have your reservation in? Fine! Now just sit back and listen to words of wisdom from one of the lucky survivors of the E-Day (exam-day) blast which all but tore apart one of the most talked about classes in the school's history. This was the class which took the concentrated French course last quarter under the able tutelage of Monsieur James L. Fleming, director of the Foreign Language Department, and Mademoiselle or Senorita Marguerita Z. Austin, French and Spanish teacher par excellence.

What class! Fourteen were originally enrolled at the beginning of the session but one dropped out, leaving that lucky combination of thirteen students to take that last exam on Friday. Of the thirteen, seven were Yankees, five native Southerners, and one—a girl!

The smoke from the blast has let up a little and I dimly perceive a few figures trudging toward me. It looks like—it is—the remnants of the once proud and cocky class with whom I once shared so many headaches and so much fun last session. Here they come—Trombetta, Vinci, Derosky, Tarravechia—Erin Go Bragh—and did ye ever see the likes of that! As fine a group of nicks from the ould sod as you'll ever see. And here comes the rest—Stoddard, Charlie Bracken, Arthur Lockard, John Both, Carnie Gooding, the Peele brothers (Dallas and Gilbert), Richard Wilson and that girl—Katie Evans.

The last time I saw them they were stretched out on the classroom floor, rendered insensible by the terrific blast. What could have revived them? They're each waving something about triumphantly! Ah, I understand perfectly now! Those are grade books they're flourishing so proudly and with the issuing of satisfactory grades, Yankee and Southerner march arm in arm happily through the smoke! That's really something worth seeing.

Dominating the Yankee lineup were such stalwarts as Alam L. Stoddard, hard-bitten ex-marine, formerly from South Africa; the fun-loving, irrepressible Sicilian born, James A. Vinci, captain in the Royal Italian Airforce through the Ethiopian and Albanian wars, who bluffed his way past Nazi guards to gain passage on the last states-bound ship leaving Italy before the start of World War II, and who served as a Marine sergeant during that conflict; and big, bluff, good-natured Ellsworth Derosky, whose brilliant basketball career was cut short when he lost a finger during the last war.

Heading the Southern contingent were John Both, quiet, good-humored, studious class leader; and you guessed it—cherchez la femme—Katherine Evans, who proved herself not only a "brain" but a swell sport as well. As the only female in a class of predatory males she underwent a terrific amount of kidding but she weathered the storm nicely all the way.

And don't overlook the teachers! There was Mademoiselle Austin, who received her B.A. from Winthrop college, her M.A. from Duke University, studied in Mexico two summers, and along with Fleming received a medal for outstanding French studies from the French ambassador. Each, however, received this award singly in different years.

Mademoiselle Austin handled the grammar part of the course and made that dull subject seem interesting with her lively, energetic teaching. Like Katie, she brought nothing but credit to the female sex with her broad-mindedness and sense of humor, which notwithstanding, did not prevent her from exercising a firm hold on class discipline.

And there was Monsieur Fleming, the easy-going (French) gentleman with the broad, slow smile, who carefully guided the class past the dangerous pitfalls of the linguaphone lessons and the not-to-easy graded French readers, and whose life reads like a novel from the pen of Richard Halliburton.

He received his B.S. from Wake Forest and his M.A. from Harvard. For a while he traveled through Europe, stopping finally in France where he remained for seven years, alternately studying philosophy, language, and phonetics; and teaching English to French students at the University of Paris. During his stay in France, he was awarded the Diplome Superieur d'Etudes Françaises from the Alliance Française, Paris, and a diploma from the Institute of Phonetics at the University of Paris.

He was working on his doctor's degree when war broke out, and he remained in Paris until the German breakthrough, fleeing then across the Spanish frontier, a few miles ahead of pursuing German troops.

We like to think back and remember the time Mlle. Austin asked the highly excitable "Bones" Lockard to pronounce some French words. "Bones" mumbled deparately for a minute, then became excited and began to stutter. "Perfect," yelled Austin, "that's the way to do it."

And the time Louis Trombetta, translating a French sentence, confused his verbs and told the class in a straightforward manner that he was a flower. I believe one class member dropped out the next day.

And taking brain-teasing "pop-tests" under Mlle. Austin, while an electric lawn mower engaged in a noisy contest with a blaring automobile horn directly below our windows, and the lovely, lilting strains of "Clare de Lune" floated through the corridors. Of listening to Fleming's interesting explanation of some of the outstanding aspects of Rabelais' Gargantua (the afternoon Katie cut class). And finally, of working on the graded French readers in class and reading such stories as the Little Tailor, Zola's The Attack On the Mill, the Man Who Slept a Hundred Years—and how we envied him towards the close of the quarter.

Competition was keen at all times, and the long hours (five hours of class work a day) and the hot afternoons sometimes ruffled ordinarily easy-going tempers, but these spells of irritation vanished swiftly before the bubbling, effervescent spirit of fun so characteristic of teachers and students alike.

Finally the merry-go-round of grammar, linguaphone lessons, and graded French readers drew to a close. E-Day came swiftly and the class retired to the French room for the final assault. The standardized tests were passed out and we bent industriously to our work. Confident smiles soon turned to worried groans, and then—the room was suddenly littered with falling bodies, the radio-active waves closed in and I blacked out. I came to, seated here before my typewriter, singing the "Marseillaise" at the top of my lungs.

It's all over now—grades came thorugh—everyone is happy—and the class has disbanded, perhaps never to reassemble again. I hate to become maudlin, but in all seriousness, I feel a deep sense of regret to see the end of this adventure. The work was arduous, but we enjoyed ourselves and learned a great deal. The entire class, teachers and students alike, were held together throughout the six weeks by a common bond of kinship, which I doubt seriously ever encountering in any class again.

And while I am still serious, I'd like to mention that this course is offered once a year, during the first summer session, when popular student demand warrants it. Its main purpose is to teach French reading in a hurry to upperclassmen, who lack a foreign language background to enable them to pass graduate requirements in other schools.

Objectives set up in the course are to finish 40 chapters of French grammar, totally close to 300 pages; to read ten graded French readers averaging 45 pages each; and to absorb ten advanced linguaphone lessons mainly to help pronunciation. The course, on the whole, however, stresses the ability to read French.

Those words of wisdom I promised you? If you are seriously considering taking this course next summer, my advice is: Take it! You'll never regret it.

Radio-active waves are closing in again and I feel myself sinking back into unconsciousness. Before I black-out, I'd like to give a final salute to the class and teachers: Au revoir, mes chers amis!

During my first few years at East Carolina Teachers College, I tried to avoid requesting any significant catalogue changes. In order to make certain, however, that our majors would be adequately prepared to teach French and Spanish at the high school level, I felt obliged to request that their requirements be changed from the state minimum of 36 quarter hours of study in one language to 45 quarter hours, and that our minor requirement be increased to 38 quarter hours. Then I added a third teacher to our department to help us teach the additional courses. Incidentally, I also yielded to the temptation to request that the one sentence in the catalogue advertising the fact that E.C.T.C. did not require a foreign language for admission be deleted. However, I never repeated that request, and no action was taken on it until 1949 when it was removed from the catalogue. In 1966 the turnaround was completed when two units of one foreign language became required for admission.

My search for the additional teacher taught me that the E.C.T.C. salary scale was not competitive. I sought far and wide and found only one person holding the desired credentials who would consider the salary I was able to offer. He spoke French fluently, with an accent I did not recognize, and he had received his Ph.D. from one of our sister institutions. Since I seemed to have no other choice, I took him on a yearly basis. He became widely known overnight, not for the brilliance of his classroom technique, but for his originality at the bridge table. Soon after he arrived in Greenville, he was asked if he played bridge. Upon replying affirmatively, he was immediately invited to substitute at a bridge club that evening for a member who had just been called out of town. He did, and his first bid of the evening was, "A king." Whereupon his partner looked up and asked, "Which suit?"

During the school year, after listening to his accent for several months, I told him that I thought that a person holding the Ph.D. should be able to get a better salary than E.C.T.C. could offer. He did, and I sought a way to get around our difficulty and still find excellent teachers more suited to our needs.

Now we felt that it was time to request that the A.B. degree at E.C.T.C. be brought up to the level of the standard liberal arts degree, which the vast majority of American colleges and universities had long ago accepted. But East Carolina Teachers College had a peculiar problem.

Dr. Robert H. Wright, the first president of this teacher-training institution, had high ideals and he wanted his future teachers to be prepared in the broad general education curriculum of the liberal arts degree, including the study of a classical or a modern foreign language. He therefore set his teacher-training curriculum in the cadre of the liberal arts degree and required the study of Latin. Later, as I said, the high schools began to favor French.

I did not disagree with President Wright's philosophy of placing the teacher training program in the A.B. degree curriculum because I knew of no profession whose members were more in need of a broad general education than that of the teachers of the youth of our nation.

When I first requested the addition of a foreign language requirement for the A.B. (liberal arts) degree, it was granted, but for some reason, it was limited to 9 quarter hours and placed among the requirements of the B.S. degree. The following year, however, the E.C.T.C. catalogue appeared with the two degrees reversed and the foreign language requirement placed under the traditionally correct degree, the A.B. (liberal arts) degree, but the requirement, cut in half, was entirely inadequate to serve its purpose. The reversal of degrees, incidentally, also removed President Wright's teacher training program from the A.B. (liberal arts) degree to the B.S. degree where no Latin or modern foreign language was required.

Soon after Dr. John D. Messick became president of East Carolina Teachers College, I spoke to him of my plan to request that the A.B. (liberal arts) degree include an adequate foreign language requirement. He did not commit himself, but said that he would get in touch with me. A few months later, apparently after consulting with others, he suggested that I wait until the following year to make my proposal. I got the impression that he agreed with my reasoning on the subject, but was not sure of faculty sentiment. Shortly thereafter, Dr. Messick stopped me on campus to tell me that his son John, at lunch that day, had said that he was learning more English in his French class than in his English class. I replied that quite often a student, in whose family good English is spoken, pays little attention to the rules of grammar which he often feels no need to learn. Then in his French class, where he has no background in the language, it becomes necessary for him to learn a few rules of grammar and, in so doing, he often reinforces the English grammar rules which he had hardly noticed in his English class.

Sometime later, Dr. Messick asked me to give a demonstration at the faculty meeting of my method of teaching a beginning French class. I did and to my pleasant surprise, following the meeting, two English teachers and one mathematics teacher asked if I would give them French lessons at an hour which all three of them happened to have free that quarter. I was flattered, honored, and delighted at the opportunity to work with them. All three were outstanding teachers, and all three attained the rank of professor in their departments.

The following year, when I approached Dr. Messick again on the subject of strengthening our A.B. degree, he scheduled consideration of my proposal for an upcoming faculty meeting. I knew that a few faculty members saw no reason for any students to "waste their time" studying a foreign language, and I expected their opposition. I knew also that those faculty members who were teaching courses which might have to be eliminated or changed to another hour might also object. And I was aware that a few heads of departments, who, to say the least, were not particularly interested in foreign languages, would now be facing the possibility of having to rework their entire departmental schedules. They might also object. But I still did not expect the faculty vote to be so close. Dr. Messick supported me, and we won by a narrow margin—so narrow, in fact, that I fully understood for the first time how much the institution needed to make that change. It was an important win, not just for the Department of Foreign Languages but for the entire institution.

Since the Middle Ages, the western world had used the A.B. (liberal arts) degree as the broad basic degree for studies in the humanities, including the study of languages. Not to require the study of foreign languages in that degree, nor in any other degree of the institution, was equivalent to eliminating a huge segment of the wisdom of mankind. It was tantamount to saying to millions of our fellow human beings, including our friends, our neighbors, and our allies, "We don't believe that you, your language, and your civilization are worthy of in-depth study."

In the years just after a second world war when the United Nations organization was being established on our soil I felt that provincialism was especially unworthy of our institution. Strengthening our A.B. (liberal arts) degree, which broadened the academic programs of the thousands of students who have graduated since that time, marked a turning point of East Carolina Teachers College away from provincialism and, along with other improvements, laid the academic foundation which permitted Dr. Messick, as president of East Carolina College, to start paving the High Road which Dr. Leo W. Jenkins would later travel, broaden and extend to greater heights.

The author and Robert Lee Humber at Atlantic Beach, 1935.

Mrs. James L. Fleming, Sr.

Louise E. Fleming

The author and Ellen Fleming.

The living room in the Fleming House.

The Fleming House

Interior view of the
Humber house, showing
portraits of Lucie Humber
(above) and Robert Lee
Humber (below).

Chapter X

It had taken four years to get an adequate foreign language requirement for the liberal arts degree accepted and properly set up in the E.C.T..C catalogue. I was no longer worried about the future of the Department of Foreign Languages. I knew that it would grow and become strong, and I was confident that I could set its sails in the right direction. Several years earlier, I had concluded that the best way to teach our students to speak the foreign language of their choice and, simultaneously, to broaden their intellectual horizons was to establish and integrate into our organization a foreign student scholarship program for each foreign language taught on our campus.

I spoke to Mr. F. D. Duncan, college treasurer, who supported our effort and helped us to get the program started. Our purpose was to bring to our campus native-speaking scholarship students for each of these languages. It was understood that these students would live in student dormitories on campus, where they would be most likely to mingle and exchange ideas with our students. We hoped that this cross-fertilization of ideas would spark new ideas and we would be able to persuade some of the best of these scholarship students to remain with us another year or so as assistants. To aid this process we also requested the foreign students to give a limited amount of time as assistants in one of our conversation classes.

For the benefit of those foreign students who were not as well prepared in English and who would probably be with us only one year, we planned and announced in the E.C.T.C. catalogue two certificates for foreign students: Certificate of American Studies and Certificate of American Studies with Distinction. Foreign students interested in qualifying for one of these certificates were advised to see the chairman of the

Department of Foreign Languages, who would help them plan the schedule of courses to be taken and explain the standards they would be expected to meet to qualify for receipt of one of the certificates.

To select our foreign scholarship students, we used the good services of the Institute of International Education, whose organization and contacts throughout the world would facilitate the assembly of data and preparation of dossiers of interested students. Marguerite and I could then examine the dossiers and select the students who we thought would be happy at East Carolina and would contribute most to our students. In studying the dossiers, I usually looked for personality, character, and scholarship in that order, because I felt that a scholar of good character who lacked personality could easily be an ineffective communicator. Furthermore, we were not offering graduate courses in foreign languages at East Carolina Teachers College. At that time our students needed to broaden their horizons before narrowing their interests.

Mlle. Geneviève Longevialle, daughter of a physician who lived in Ussel, France, was one of the first students we selected. She was a delightful, rosy-cheeked young lady with a good command of English. She made acquaintances easily and got along very well with our students, although she had difficulty understanding why Americans felt that they had to ride everywhere, even to go downtown, just a few blocks away. After she had been on campus a month or so and was apparently becoming accustomed to our ways and to our southern speech, I accompanied her to a number of ladies' book clubs, whose members had expressed a desire to meet her.

The first club we visited, however, was not a book club but a ladies' club in the county, whose members had asked that they be the first club in their area to receive her. Their meeting place was a spacious cabin in the woods near a crossroads some miles from Greenville. Soon after we arrived at the cabin, spoke to a few ladies, and took our seats, the chairperson tapped firmly on the table and called for the meeting to come to order. Silence suddenly fell over the large room. The chairperson then turned to the lady sitting at the table beside her and intoned in a strong monotone, "Will the secretary read the minutes of the last meeting?" The little lady quickly opened her notebook, fingered through the pages, and started reading. I glanced at Geneviève because I knew that this procedure would surprise her. She was paying strict attention and listening intently. A moment later, however, the little secretary read the name of one of the club members and suddenly stopped and exclaimed, "Oh, she's dead," and quickly flipped more pages and started reading again. Geneviève glanced at me. I looked down, and we both managed to keep a straight face.

When the business meeting was terminated, I was asked to introduce "our special guest." After placing a map of France where everyone could see it, I described briefly our foreign student scholarship program. Then I explained that Mlle. Longevialle would use the map to show where in France her hometown was located, but that she would talk only briefly about her family and the area where she lives, so there would be ample time for questions following her remarks.

Geneviève was a member of a large family and she was a well-informed young lady with a good, clear mind. Her remarks were direct and frank and when the questions were asked, she was equally direct and frank in her responses. There were many questions asked, but those that I still remember after thirty-five years are the following:

Question: Do you have many ladies' clubs like ours in France?
Answer: No.
Question: How do you get together with your friends?
Answer: I pick up the telephone and call a few friends to meet me at the café. We prefer a small group because it's difficult to discuss anything in a large group.
Question: What do you call a small group?
Answer: Not more than five or six. The more persons present, the more likely they are to split into a number of small groups and all talk at the same time.
Question: Do French women wear as many colors as we?
Answer: Yes, but not at the same time. I find I can blend two or three colors at a time, but the more colors I add the less likely I am to retain a feeling of harmony among them.
Question: What kind of a man would you choose for a husband?

Answer: One who is intelligent.
Question: I mean blond or brunette?
Answer: That wouldn't matter if he were intelligent.

Geneviève's answer to the last question surprised many and reminded me to add to my French civilization reading list Salvador de Madariaga's *Français, Anglais et Espagnoles*, in which the author generalizes that the Englishman is a man of action, meaning that when action is needed to be taken, he acts, then "muddles his way through"; the Spaniard acts on a passion; and the Frenchman is a man of thought.

The foreign students enjoyed visiting the ladies' book clubs, which varied from groups which were definitely intellectually inclined to those whose delightful conversationalists appeared to be more interested in the social gathering with friends than in books. The former carefully selected outstanding books, which they read, reported on, and discussed. The latter were more likely to list the books to be read during the year, then pass them from member to member until some had been misplaced or lost or just gone with the wind. The students, who were always graciously received, enjoyed their visits inside American homes and were happy to get a glimpse of the activities and thoughts of American women.

Many foreign scholarship students spent one or more years on our campus, and a few remained several years. Our American students, during their four-year period of study at E.C.T.C. (later East Carolina College and East Carolina University), were thus able to enjoy the privilege of getting to know several foreign students. Sound international friendships developed, and a few marriages took place.

A glimpse of four of the young ladies from foreign countries who were with us during the 1960s will give some notion of the type of persons we were fortunate to bring to our campus. Three of these came from Spanish-speaking countries and one from France.

Señorita Julia Escalona, who came to us with a teaching degree from the University of Santiago, Chile, earned a master's degree at East Carolina College and remained with us several years as a Spanish instructor. Today Julia is teaching Spanish in Phoebus Senior High School in Hampton, Virginia, where she and her husband, Bill Turner, a former East Carolina student, enjoy the luxury of a two-income family. Their daughter, Sonia, entered East Carolina University as a freshman in August of 1987.

Señorita Raquel Taño received her teacher's degree from the Escuela Normal de Camaguey and took graduate studies at the University of Havana before becoming a refugee teacher in the United States. After receiving her master's degree from the University of North Carolina at Chapel Hill, she returned to Greenville, where she and Mr. Arch E. Manning were married. Arch is an alumnus of East Carolina University and a teacher-consultant with the North Carolina Department of Education. They are living in Greenville and Raquel in 1988 is still enjoying teaching Spanish at East Carolina University.

Señorita Maria Haendel, who received her Bachiller en Notariado y Abogacia from the Instituto Alfredo Vazquez Acevedo in Montevideo, Uruguay, earned her master's degree at East Carolina University. During that year she met and fell in love with Bill Koonce, an East Carolina University student from Kinston, North Carolina. Then upon the sudden death of her father, Maria returned home.

The weeks that followed became an eternity to Maria and Bill, until suddenly, as if by miracle, Bill became a dashing Spanish prince, took flight to Montevideo, met Maria's family, married Maria, and came back to earth at East Carolina University with his lovely bride, who joyfully worked as an instructor of Spanish until Bill completed his degree.

Their Christmas letter of 1986 reveals so much of the beauty of their lives and of their family that I asked Maria if I might include that letter in this volume.

Xmas, 1986

Dear Friends:

This means of communication might be corny, but it is practical and effective, and, after all, isn't that the American way? Since this has been an unusually eventful year for us, I bow to my adoptive country's ingenuity, and will share with all of you the high-lights of 1986.

The motto that had been referred to us before, "Never a dull moment at the Koonces," could not have a better application than it did this year, and we are deeply thankful that everything has been positive and wonderful.

Let us begin with the youngest member of our clan, Maria-Paula. Our beautiful daughter (outside as well as inside) was selected Miss Teenage Hispana de Broward 1986,

104

and with the sovereignty, she won some very attractive prizes. One of these was a trip to Puerto Rico, which she shared with her parents in celebration of their 24th wedding anniversary. It has all been a beautiful experience for her and for us in many ways. Maria-Paula graduated from high school this year and took a semester off her studies to work, save some money, and to travel to Uruguay. She is there now, spending two months with the family, renewing her fluency of Spanish, and living some specially unique moments that should enrichen her personality and her life. When she returns after the new year, she will begin her course work in the nursing program at Broward Community College.

But this is not all that happened to Maria-Paula. She also managed to fall in love and to become engaged. This she did best of all. We are all delighted with our future son, Scott. Suffice it to say that had we been able to design the perfect prince for our treasure, we would have come short of the reality. Scott faithfully attended Spanish classes taught by his future mother-in-law to prepare himself for his visit to Uruguay, where he is now spending the holidays, and, no doubt, enjoying every minute of it. History really repeats itself, as it seems like yesterday that Bill underwent the same baptism by fire to marry me - but it was not yesterday; it was almost 25 years ago.

Now about Michael. He was no less active than his sister this year. As most of you know, he took the most drastic step in his life: he married a wonderful and beautiful girl, Patti, in August. After some very suspenseful moments wondering if the U.S. Navy (which seem to consider that their plans were a priority) Michael was able to be present, and the wedding was lovely: the newlyweds enjoyed all the families that came for the occasion, honeymooned in Cancun, and are now playing house . . . and discovering the realities of life in their cozy apartment in Jacksonville. An addition to that family is Buddy (a playful puppy).

Age before beauty? Yes. Bill had to make a decision concerning his work, and after a long debate, he accepted an unusual opportunity. Since he is considered the expert in power supplies within the electronic industry, he was asked to install a system in Martin Marietta, in Ocala. This meant that he would be on loan to this company for the duration, and, of course, it implied weekly commuting. Since then, we discovered the pleasures of escaping some weekends to his neat trailer under the pine trees in this pastoral corner of Florida. Bill travels home to Ft. Lauderdale some weekends, and I, Maria, visit him on others, and we love the variety and the adventure.

Now it's my turn (I suppose you know who the author of this biographical masterpiece is). After six years of intellectual racing, I finally made it this year. I defended my dissertation, and received my Doctorate in Education from F.A.U. in February. Immediately, although not directly as a consequence, I was offered a position as Curriculum Specialist in Foreign Languages for Broward County. With mixed feelings, hating to part with colleagues and students at Western High, I accepted. I found that I have grown rapidly in my profession since then. I do love my work tremendously, and find it challenging, varied and rewarding in every way. Bill organized an unforgettable celebration for me at Key Lime (still one of our favorite spots on earth), and the family and friends who had supported and encouraged me through the years have rejoiced with me (maybe glad not to have to put up any longer with the trials, tribulations, moanings, and groanings that go along with doctoral work). I treated myself to an old dream: a gold Le Baron convertible, which I adore to drive.

We are thankful that our elders had a healthy year, and that we had unusual opportunities to visit them. Both the Letchworths and the Koonces came down three times this year: for M.P.'s graduation, for Michael's wedding, and just to enjoy some more sunny Florida. Bill's sister, Marion, was also here for the wedding, which was a treat to all of us. Eduardo came for the graduation and the wedding, and we will be spending the Xmas holidays with him in California, a big first, that we are excited about. Could it be that my playboy brother might finally have some commitment to announce? Mama came from Uruguay for most of the summer events. Unfortunately, she had a hard time with two delicate operations, but, "all is well that ends well." Her usual stamina and spirit have allowed her to beat the odds and become her own active bubbly self again. She is now holding court for M.P. and Scott, and surely loving every minute of it.

Another special visitor this Summer from the peanut gallery was my nephew, Marcelo-Enrique. At age 11, he traveled alone and spent the month of July with us—a month packed with experiences: a week at the keys, Disney World, Epcot, Ocala, and Ft. Lauderdale. We were delighted to enjoy his sweet, sensitive personality, his adorable good manners, and his excitement at all the new things that he was living.

This year brought some endings. Stephanie Plesek, who had spent her senior year with us, moved on to her folks.

106

We are the richer for having had her, and she left us with lovely and funny memories. Our children are now adults (for most extents and purposes). But the endings also mark wonderful beginnings. The transfer of the Xmas decorations and the trimming of the tree from our home to Michael and Patti's this year is, I think, symbolic of this normal process. Our growing independence and fulfillment in our lives and professions, and, above all, the pattern of love, respect, and closeness that is now solidly established among us all, the true friendships that are lasting, and the health and good fortune that we continue to enjoy are more than enough rewards for the passage of time. We are, indeed, grateful!

WE WISH YOU ALL THE BEST FROM THE BOTTOM OF OUR HEARTS!

The Koonces

Mlle. Catherine LaBaume, who came to us with a bachelor's degree and a commercial M.A. from Paris, earned an M.A. at East Carolina College and remained with us as an instructor of French for a number of years. While teaching in the Department of Foreign Languages, she volunteered to work with me in an experimental class of spoken French in the elementary grades. At the invitation of Mrs. Myrtle Clark, we started our project in her third grade class at the Wahl-Coates School.

The first day of class, we spoke only enough English to orient the students, then we spoke French aided by an ample supply of expressive bodily and facial movements. When we entered the classroom, Mrs. Clark presented Mademoiselle LaBaume and me to the class. I lowered a map of Europe and pointed to France, saying in English, "The people of this country, France (which I gave the French pronunciation), are a democratic people, very much like us, but they speak a different language. It is a polite language, and they are a polite people. When they meet in the morning, they shake hands and extend greetings to one another." Then I approached Mlle. LaBaume saying, "Bonjour, mademoiselle." Shaking my hand, she replied, "Bonjour, monsieur." We repeated the routine a few times in order to give the students every opportunity to hear clearly the sounds we were making and also to observe that the handshake was characteristically one pump of the arm. Then we reversed the order. Mademoiselle LaBaume ap-

107

proached me saying, "Bonjour, monsieur." Shaking her hand, I replied, "Bonjour, mademoiselle." Then speaking in French and making appropriate gestures toward the class, I asked Mademoiselle LaBaume to say "Bonjour" and shake hands with each of the students and to wait for the reply, "Bonjour, mademoiselle."

While Mlle. LaBaume was making the rounds, I paid close attention to each response. I noticed particularly a little football player with a strong quarterback voice, but with a relatively short attention span. When it became my turn to greet the students individually, I decided not to call on them in their seating order. I went directly to my little football player, held out my hand and said, "Bonjour, monsieur." Confidently, he smiled, shook my hand and in a big, clear voice, he said, "Bonjour, mademoiselle." The class screamed with laughter at his error and, of course, I vociferously protested, "Mais non monsieur, je ne suis pas mademoiselle, je suis monsieur." Pointing at a girl, I said "mademoiselle," at a boy, "monsieur," at myself, "monsieur." Then pointing at my little quarterback and raising my voice to form a question I asked, "Mademoiselle?" He quickly responded, "Monsieur, monsieur."

That year, in the Wahl-Coates French class, my little quarterback truly lengthened his attention span. He knew that when I asked a question and didn't get a correct response, sooner or later I would call on him. He usually gave the correct answer, but when he looked down at his desk, I knew that he didn't know the answer and occasionally I let him off the hook.

Mlle. LaBaume and I continued that experiment in the third grade for a number of years. We understood and appreciated the advantage of starting with young minds which, like little sponges, draw in everything without stopping to ask, "Why do they talk like that?" But if you wait just one year longer and begin the study of a foreign language in the fourth grade, the students will surely ask that question, and it will retard their progress in the foreign language.

Eight years later, on the first day of class at East Carolina University, I was trying to determine how much French my new students understood. One young lady's French sounded like French, not like a translation from English. In fact, her French was so much more natural than that of the others that I asked where she had attended high school. She replied,

"Rose High School in Greenville." "And who was your French teacher at Rose High?" I asked. "I didn't take French in high school," she replied. "Then where did you learn your French?" She smiled and responded, "From you and Mlle. LaBaume."

One experience does not justify general conclusions, but following my experience with the French class in the third grade, I was convinced that the best way to develop a good speaking ability in a foreign language is to start at the earliest possible age with a good native teacher of the language.

The presence of our French class in the third grade of one school stirred considerable interest throughout the area in other schools. Parents, teachers, and children tried to persuade us to start classes in their schools and, of course, had it been possible, we would have done so. We knew what it would mean to those children to be able to build, in the very foundation of their educational structure, a second language facility which would open great vistas of new worlds which would otherwise probably never be opened to them. We were familiar with the wealth of games and songs and poems and fables and stories and art available in that incredible storehouse of French literature and culture, with which we could enrich the lives of children who learn to speak and understand French at an early age.

The great literature of the world belongs to all mankind. We are all born individuals—no two of us alike. Not even identical twins have identical thoughts. We are all endowed with the incredible talent of a human brain of infinite potential and we have only one short life to develop that brain to the level of intelligence that will permit us to enjoy it. Our education begins the day of our birth. Why shouldn't all children be given, as early in life as possible, more than a one-language, one-civilization view of the world?

Why must human beings be educationally and intellectually limited to a dangerously narrow one-nation bias? Why shouldn't children be introduced to the clarity, beauty, and charm of a great second language and its civilization while they are young enough to absorb it without bias? They could make it their own second window onto this international world in which we must all try to live together in peace.

In European countries, where it is customary for children to study a second language six to eight years, many young people become bilingual. In France each year a great number of young French women travel from France to England, where they teach French in English schools and homes. And, of course, a like number of young English women go to France to teach English in French schools and homes.

The announcement made in March of 1987 by the North Carolina Board of Education, that beginning in 1993 the students of the North Carolina public schools in grades kindergarten through five will be required to study a second language, and that the schools will also be required to make second language courses available to students in grades six through twelve, was a glorious invitation to the children of this state to become bilingual and to open wide a second window onto the world.

The following article taken from the Greenville *Daily Reflector* of Thursday, June 30, 1988 is an example of East Carolina University's continuous effort to anticipate and meet the needs of its students.

Twenty-one East Carolina University students, accompanied by Professor Karine Sparrow-Ginter, are in Paris where they will participate in a five-week program of study at the Sorbonne.

Group members left Monday aboard an Air France flight to Paris. Most participants will reside in student lodgings across from the Luxembourg Gardens in the heart of the Latin Quarter, on the famed Left Bank.

They will attend classes in the French language at the Cours de Langue et de Civilisation Francaise which, according to Ms. Sparrow-Ginter, is the "oldest and most prestigious part of the university."

"The Sorbonne was founded in the 13th century and has long been a mecca for international students," she said.

Students will be placed in classes of various levels, according to the results of an initial placement test. Each will receive three hours of college credit for language study from ECU and a certificate from the Sorbonne.

The students will receive additional credits for an afternoon French civilization class, which includes lectures, cultural readings and guided visits to museums, monuments and chateaux in and around Paris. Particular emphasis will be placed on French history, art and architecture.

The ECU-Sorbonne study program, now in its second year, has attracted students from Meredith College, the University of North Carolina at Chapel Hill, North Carolina State University and Appalachian State University as well as ECU, along with some "non-traditional students who are satisfying a life-long dream of studying in France."

Pitt County residents participating in the Sorbonne program include former French teacher Sally Bramley; her daughter, Susan Bramley; Judi Orbach, an elementary education graduate who is taking courses in French for possible use in elementary level foreign language teaching, and Dora Snow, an English teacher who is preparing for future teaching assignments in French classes.

Chapter XI

In 1945 when Miss Marguerite Austin and I constituted the faculty of the Department of Foreign Languages of East Carolina Teachers College, we started with a total yearly enrollment of less than 200 students at a time when the enrollment of the college was 1,184. Our obvious immediate task was to create interest in foreign languages and try to break the prevalent indifferent attitude toward the study of foreign languages on the campus of East Carolina Teachers College. The liberal arts degree, which is normally the foundation stone of a foreign language department, lacked, at E.C.T.C., its foreign language requirement, and was thus a stumbling block to us. It required four years of diligent effort on our part to convert that stumbling block into a solid foundation on which we could build a department.

Marguerite took a full teaching load from the start and voluntarily accepted many assignments which, under normal circumstances, would not have been asked of her. Notwithstanding the absence of professional secretarial help, I tried to do the administrative work and carry a full teaching load. As the department began to grow and add teachers, however, I was forced to reduce my teaching load, although I preferred teaching to administrative work.

The French exhibit, followed by the arrival on campus of a few of our foreign scholarship students and the return of ex-servicemen from overseas, helped to focus some attention on our foreign language program. It was, however, the slow but steady growth of the department, plus the strong support of President John D. Messick, that enabled us to persuade a reluctant East Carolina Teachers College faculty to add an adequate foreign language requirement to its A.B. degree, thus giving that degree the stature of a true liberal arts degree. This change, noted by our colleagues throughout the

112

state, removed one of the reasons for criticism often leveled at the academic standards of E.C.T.C. at South Atlantic Modern Language Association meetings, where I went to seek qualified teachers to join our staff. This change also assured us of steady growth in the future and enabled us to concentrate on the quality of that growth. Incidentally, this success apparently gave Marguerite and me greater confidence in the future. We both became married that spring: Marguerite to George Perry of the music faculty and I, to one of Marguerite's closest friends, Ellen Rion Caldwell of the mathematics faculty.

We set the stage for the strengthening of our departmental program by giving a series of standard exams with national norms. The results revealed that our French students were above the national norm, but that our Spanish students were slightly below the national norm. These results lead us to establish a program of standard exams at two levels in all languages throughout the department. The continuation of this two-level exam series over a period of several years was time-consuming and a burden to our faculty, but it enabled me to locate a few weaknesses which I endeavored to correct. Meanwhile our standards rose to a very satisfactory level, and we limited the use of standard exams with national norms to the intermediate level in all foreign languages.

This effort was followed by a departmental study of all courses offered in the department, for the purpose of locating weaknesses and recommending procedures for strengthening the foreign language curriculum. This study resulted in the change of title and content of one course and the addition of two literature courses.

We requested a modern electronic language laboratory. Although turned down by the State Board of Higher Education, our request was granted by the state legislature, and our laboratory was installed a year later. This addition enabled our faculty to place greater emphasis on the spoken approach to the study of the language.

The number of quarter hours required of French and Spanish majors and minors was again increased, this time from 45 to 50 quarter hours for majors and from 38 to 45 quarter hours for minors.

In harmony with the institution's logo and policy "To Serve," we offered French and Spanish courses at Camp Le-Jeune and at Cherry Point, military bases in eastern North

Carolina. The demand for Spanish at Camp LeJeune was so great that two full-time instructors had to be assigned to Camp LeJeune.

Following the Sputnik affair, we published a brochure designed to draw more student interest to foreign language study, and we offered Russian on campus and at Camp LeJeune. We set up a class in spoken French at the Wahl-Coates Elementary School and added a French course for majors who might wish to work with Mlle. LaBaume and native French scholarship students who were then aiding in the teaching of French in the elementary grades.

Along with all the departments of the institution, we conducted a departmental self-study. Our self-study resulted in a broadening and strengthening of our course offerings and the appointment of French and Spanish graduate committees for the purpose of planning graduate programs.

By the year 1964, my nineteenth year as chairman of the Department of Foreign Languages, the Office of Personnel of East Carolina College sent to us our first professional secretary. At that time we had an annual enrollment in foreign languages of 3,768 students and a faculty of fifteen members, of whom five held Ph.D.'s and five others were bilingual or native speakers of the language they were teaching. Mrs. Ann Molic had moved to North Carolina with her husband, Walter, who had come to Greenville to join the Voice of America. She applied for a secretarial position at East Carolina College, and Mr. Worth Baker referred her to me. Mrs. Molic was an excellent typist, a neat, personable office manager, and a delightful person to work with. The only advice I remember giving Mrs. Molic was really not advice at all, but merely the names of several well-informed campus secretaries who, I knew, would be happy to help guide her through the intricacies and peculiarities of our way of getting things done on the E.C.C. campus. Although Ann was later offered other positions on campus, she turned them down and remained with the Department of Foreign Languages until she retired, a member of an elite group of administrative secretaries, in 1986.

In the 1960s the Department of Foreign Languages was growing at a faster rate than the college as a whole. Foreign language study at E.C.C. was no longer an enigma to be avoided but recognized on campus as an interesting way to learn to communicate with great numbers of our fellow men throughout this world of which we are a part. Although holding steadfastly to the great traditions of the past, the Department of Foreign Languages had turned its back on the narrow provincial view of the world and was quietly laying a strong liberal arts foundation for the future.

Traditional foreign language requirements such as those for prelegal, predental and premedical students, had long since been placed in the college catalogue. The English department, responding to one of my earliest requests on campus, had added a foreign language requirement for its majors, who were planning to teach English in the public schools. Those students would henceforth be able to make valid comparisons and thus sharpen and broaden their knowledge of their own language. Many other departments such as speech, drama, art, vocal music, geography and history were requiring or recommending the study of foreign languages. Dr. Browning added a foreign language requirement to one of the degrees of the School of Business. After his School of Business became nationally accredited, he told me that the foreign language requirement had been well received by the accreditation committee. Their reasoning seemed to have been based, in part, on a belief that American businessmen had finally become convinced that they could do more business with the proud businessmen of the great civilized nations of the world if they showed more interest in their culture and tried to speak their language, rather than expecting everybody to speak English with them.

By 1966, the annual student enrollment of the Department of Foreign Languages had soared to 6,004 and its faculty to twenty-six members. The department was bursting at the seams. Foreign language classes were being taught in Old Austin, Rawl, Education and Psychology, and Graham buildings. I had previously requested that the department be brought together with its laboratory facilities in one building. Now that our need had become more obvious on campus, I decided to make that request again before the 1967-69 biennium.

When I studied my departmental growth projection charts and extended them to 1970, the year of my retirement, instead of showing the leveling off which I was beginning to anticipate, the charts revealed that the Department of Foreign Languages would require thirty-six teachers by that date. That meant the addition of ten new teachers who, in 1970, when I retired, would have to adjust or readjust to a new chairperson who had not selected them. There was, however, a good and appropriate alternative which could solve the problem, because the Department of Foreign Languages, which has inherent language division lines, had grown to such an extent that it now needed to be divided.

We had built a good undergraduate department and our graduate programs, in the planning stages, would be completed and approved by the State Board of Higher Education by January 20, 1970. Meanwhile, some members of our faculty, alert to the challenge of new opportunities, had already developed and directed two federally financed National Defense Education Act Institutes, and a third NDEA Institute and an Education Professions Development Act Institute would be held before 1970.

In brief, if the Department of Foreign Languages were not divided before 1970, a new chairperson would be faced with the task of directing a French undergraduate department plus the possibility of an infant French graduate division, a Spanish undergraduate department plus the possibility of an infant Spanish graduate division; a developing German undergraduate department; and directing a growing Russian program. Moreover, if the chairperson followed in my footsteps, he or she would also teach two courses each quarter and attend committee meetings on campus and all the professional foreign language meetings necessary to locate, interview, evaluate, and hire the French, Spanish, German, and Russian teachers which our projection charts revealed that we would need. Of course, the chairperson would also inherit the unresolved problem of bringing all the foreign language divisions, their faculties, and students together in one building with our language laboratory facilities.

In the light of this overwhelming picture, I saw little prospect of finding a good, conscientious language professor who would be willing to tackle such a task until after the Department of Foreign Languages had been divided. I decided, therefore, that it was time for me to recommend that the department be divided and that chairpersons for the new divisions be selected. I felt that the three remaining years before my retirement should give us ample time to set in motion a plan of transition which would lead smoothly into a new era of foreign language chairmanship at East Carolina. Meanwhile, Mrs. Molic and I would expect to make ourselves available to the new chairpersons, help in coordinating their work and offer any assistance they might need.

The question thus became: How should the department be divided? From a scholarly point of view of studies leading to graduate degrees, I was inclined to favor the grouping of languages in families, such as Romance languages, Germanic languages, and Slavic languages. But, at East Carolina, more than 80 percent of our foreign language students at that time were taking French and Spanish, two Romance languages, and that was where we needed to make a division.

Historically, students entering Romance languages in college had already taken two years of Latin in high school. This early study of the mother tongue was an excellent background for the study of French and Spanish, and the method of teaching these languages, at that time, was usually the grammar-translation method, leading to a reading knowledge of the language.

But times had changed. Just after the first decade of this century when Robert Lee Humber decided that he wanted to become a Rhodes scholar and sought to take Latin, he learned that the Greenville high school curriculum had been modernized, and the ancient language, Latin, had been replaced by the modern language, French. That trend was beginning to sweep the country and students, unaware of the value of studying the mother tongue, began to ask, "Why study a dead language that is no longer spoken in order to learn a living modern language?" Whether right or wrong, high schools continued to drop Latin from their curriculums and students began entering college less prepared to enjoy Romance language studies. After two years of foreign language study in college, they often bitterly complained that they still really couldn't speak the language.

Without questioning any method of teaching or suggesting any changes, I submitted a request for a modern electronic foreign language laboratory. President Messick supported me, and East Carolina College became the first state-supported educational institution in North Carolina to install a modern electronic language laboratory. In that laboratory the student could silently read the text while listening to a native speaker reading the same material. The student could read the same material aloud, recording his or her own voice on the same tape, and then play back the tape to make comparisons. The laboratory library kept available a great variety of linguistic exercises designed to guide the student through the mental gymnastics needed to develop the basic patterns of speech leading to a speaking ability of the language. We had also brought to our campus foreign scholarship students who could help transform the mechanical drills of the lab into living relationships. By vote of our faculty, we changed to textbooks which placed greater emphasis on the spoken word.

Under the direction of native French-speaking teachers and with the assistance of native foreign scholarship students, we had also developed an experimental French program in the Wahl-Coates Elementary School, which we continued long enough for us to conclude that this was not the easiest, but it was certainly the best approach to the development of a good speaking ability in a foreign language.

The changes we had been making at East Carolina College were in harmony with the changing attitude toward the study of foreign languages in America. Berlitz schools, emphasizing the spoken language, were becoming popular. Outstanding colleges and universities were sponsoring summer language institutes with native-speaking visiting professors, stressing the spoken language. American-trained foreign language teachers who had had less opportunity to develop a good speaking ability of the foreign language were giving up their summer vacations in order to attend one of the institutes or to spend the summer in Mexico or in France. In other words, a speaking knowledge of a second language was becoming more important to the American people. Before World War I, Americans had seen little reason to study a foreign language. After two world wars and two noble efforts to establish world peace, Americans began to understand that the failure to win the peace was not entirely the fault of their leaders.

When Robert Lee Humber was campaigning across this nation in behalf of world federation in the 1940s, he was astounded to find among legislators in some states those who opposed sharing the great American idea of federation by quoting George Washington's advice to his infant nation nearly two hundred years earlier, to avoid entangling alliances. Little did they know that at that moment, the United States of America was already a party, and probably wisely so, to more international alliances than any other nation on earth.

Following World War II, the American people began to understand that there could be no world peace until the people of the world could do more communicating with one another. The study of foreign languages at the beginning of this century was still essentially the domain of the scholar, the elite, or the wealthy. When the servicemen returned home in the mid-1940s, a speaking knowledge of a second language became a legitimate interest of the American populace. The GI's had not been American tourists trying to see Europe in two weeks. They had spent two or three years stationed in foreign lands in many parts of the world, where they lived among the inhabitants long enough to become truly interested in them, their families, and their ideas. Even in wartime, they had gotten a deeper, more accurate understanding of the people they met than tourists ever will. Many GI's had made a serious effort to learn the language of the country where they were stationed.

In America, the older generation, which had not gone to war, might still be thinking in terms of Washington's entangling alliances, but not the war generation. Through their long experience in great nations and in less well known countries which they used to call strange, far away places, they had matured and returned home with a much broader understanding of life and of mankind. Their great effort back home to extend democracy to include all Americans was, to many of them, a necessary step before they could think of trying to extend democracy through world law to their newfound friends and neighbors overseas. But the idea was planted in the hearts and minds of many of them.

In deciding how to divide the Department of Foreign Languages, many of these thoughts had come to my mind. I wanted the division to be in harmony with the changes that had taken place in the teaching of foreign languages and with the new attitude in America toward the study of foreign languages. I wanted our students to continue to receive a sound basic knowledge of the structure of the language and the beauty of its literature, but I also wanted them to be given every opportunity available to develop a good, correct speaking ability of the language. We had outgrown our first electronic lab, and I had already submitted a request for five new modern electronic language laboratories, which I knew would not be wastefully installed in an old building some distance from the rest of the department. I had asked Dr. James L. White, professor of business, to seek information in Washington, D.C., on the availability of federal funds for the construction and equipping of foreign language laboratories. His reply follows:

EAST CAROLINA COLLEGE
Greenville, North Carolina

M E M O R A N D U M

DATE: October 13, 1965
TO: James L. Fleming
FROM: James L. White

I took your letter with me to Washington last week and tried to find someone with some answers to your problem. The picture does not look too bright at this point under existing legislation.

I talked to a Mr. Jay DuVon in the Bureau of Higher Education. He stated that it would be far easier to get money under the Higher Education Facilities Act for building a language building and equipping it than it would be to get money to expand existing facilities. (You really have another problem, I believe, in that you are restricted in space in your building to develop additional language laboratories, n'est-ce pas?) Mr. DuVon stated that under the HEFA the college could get up to 75 per cent of the total cost of a Modern Foreign Language building (loan and grant combined) and the College would have to put up at least 25 per cent of the total cost.

Quite frankly, I couldn't find anybody in that maze of offices who could advise me on pending or proposed legislation under which we might apply for college language labs. I'll keep trying—and I'll let you know.

I pictured the entire Department of Foreign Languages in a new building in which the language groups would be separated from one another, i.e., the French professors' offices, the French classrooms, and the French lab rooms would all open onto a French environmental area which could encourage additional conversation in the language. I pictured a similar arrangement for each language group, knowing, of course, that the German and Russian groups might have to wait until the enrollment justified complete separation. I felt that such an arrangement would not only meet the needs of the scholarly student seeking advanced degrees, but also those of the vast new generation of foreign language under-graduates, many of whom might be interested essentially in learning to speak the foreign language. I therefore submitted a request that the Department of Foreign Languages be divided into a French division, a Spanish division, and a German and Russian division, and that a chairperson be sought for each division.

While members of the administration were seeking qualified chairpersons holding the proper credentials, Dr. John Howell, then dean of the School of Arts and Sciences, asked me to represent him at South Atlantic Modern Language Association. Sometime later, when I learned that none of us had met with success, I sent the following short letter to Dr. Howell:

December 1, 1966

Dr. John M. Howell, Dean
School of Arts and Sciences
East Carolina College

Dear Dr. Howell :

In recommending that the Department of Foreign Languages be divided into three departments within the School of Arts and Sciences, I have been scrupulously careful not to influence the selection of new chairmen.

Since representing you at SAMLA and interviewing interested persons, I have reached the conclusion that we have on our present staff far better candidates for these positions than any I met.

I feel, therefore, that I would be derelict in my duty if I did not at least suggest to you that I would be happy to review the credentials and discuss with you the work of any member of our current staff whom you might wish to consider for one of these positions.

Sincerely yours,

James L. Fleming
Chairman

JLF:afm

Meanwhile, as a reminder of our report of the previous year, depicting our crowded condition and requesting five new language laboratories in a new building, I sent the following note related to budgetary planning for the 1967-69 biennium to Mr. F. D. Duncan, vice-president and business manager:

January 14, 1966

Mr. F. D. Duncan
Vice President and Business Manager
East Carolina College

Dear Mr. Duncan:

The enclosed copies of data sent to Dean Williams are related to budgetary planning for the 1967-69 biennium.

I would call your attention particularly to the following:

1. The present crowded condition of the Department of Foreign Languages. The enclosed departmental growth chart should give some idea of the space crisis already upon us, since the five classrooms presently assigned to the department, are already scheduled from 8:00 A.M. to 5:00 P.M. daily, Monday through Friday, and there still remain approximately 1/3 of our classes to be scheduled in other buildings across the campus. This quarter (Winter 1965-66) for example, the Department of Foreign Languages is holding classes in Old Austin, Rawl, Education and Psychology, and Graham buildings.

2. The inadequacy of our present laboratory facilities. On the chart, you will note our estimated need of five 30-booth laboratories by the year 1968-69.

3. My recommendation that we start planning without delay for the division of the Department of Foreign Languages into three separate departments. This recommendation is made principally for reasons of efficiency and is predicated upon assurance that additional funds will be made available for the secretarial staffs of the newly created departments.

4. My recommendation that this division go into effect in the fall of 1967.

5. My recommendation that we plan new quarters for the department (or departments) of Foreign Languages in a new classroom building. I believe it would be inefficient and wasteful to do otherwise in the light of the new laboratories and other language teaching equipment to be installed and used by teachers and students of French, Spanish and German.

Sincerely yours,

James L. Fleming, Chairman
Department of Foreign Languages

CC: Dr. Robert W. Williams
Assistant Dean

About six months later, following the suggestion of Dr. Leo W. Jenkins, I sent a projection chart and the following letter to Dr. Robert Holt, vice-president and Dean:

June 17, 1966

Dr. Robert L. Holt
Vice President and Dean
East Carolina College

Dear Dr. Holt:

In response to Dr. Jenkins' suggestions of Tuesday afternoon, June 14, I am enclosing a copy of a projection sheet which we developed last January to which we have added one column advancing the projection to 1970. In addition to the statistics in this column concerning the number of students, teachers, and classrooms, etc., needed, you will see newly added footnotes on the page of comments accompanying this chart referring to anticipated graduate programs and the development of a minor in German.

During the years depicted on this chart, we have been strengthening the undergraduate offerings of the department. To accomplish this, we have made use of departmental exams and national exams, and on two occasions, we have made rather decisive changes in our departmental offerings. We have also held one NDEA institute and several work-shops for in-service teachers. We now feel that we are ready to move toward the establishment of a

123

master's program in French and Spanish. A committee within the department has been appointed to make the necessary preliminary studies in this direction.

Sincerely yours,

James L. Fleming, Chairman
Department of Foreign Languages

JLF:afm
Enclosures

When the administration was finally able to make its decision with reference to my request, I was happy that two chairpersons, Dr. Joseph Fernandez and Dr. Henry Wanderman, had been selected from our staff. Of course, I would have preferred that Romance languages be divided into departments of French and Spanish, and in that case that Dr. Fernandez be named chairperson of Spanish and Mrs. Marguerite A. Perry be named chairperson of French. As for myself, I was selfishly delighted because my work load, which had been quite a burden, would at last be considerably lightened, and the new chairpersons, who knew our system, would need little help from me.

What pleased me most, however, was that I would be able to enjoy the teaching of a few of my favorite courses before I retired in 1970. I knew that certain courses which I had taught in the past were valuable to future teachers of French, and when I received a letter from a former student telling me so, a warm glow flickered in my old heart, as it did again in June of 1986 when I received this letter, sixteen years after my retirement:

High Point, North Carolina
Wednesday, June 11

Dear Mr. Fleming,

You won't believe what happened today! While going through some old materials, I came across my class notes for French 320 (Civilization) which I took with you in 1956. Could it have been *thirty* years ago? I was impressed again with the content of the course and with what I learned that I still use. Thanks again for your inspiration.

On June 24 I leave to accompany a group of 9 students and 2 other adults on the enclosed itinerary. Terrorists or not—here we come! We'll return 11 July.

Please give my kindest regards to Mrs. Fleming. I hope that your summer will be delightfully pleasant.

Amicalement,
Ann

Ann Mayo Morris made a grade of A on every course she took at East Carolina College, except one. That was a class in swimming, which I advised her to take. During her years as a French teacher, she has taken six groups of her students to France. She reared two daughters who graduated from Duke University several years ago and also cared for her husband who was a diabetic. When her mother died a few years ago, Ann told me that there were two persons who always thought that she could accomplish anything. "They were," she said, "my Mother and you."

Chapter XII

After getting settled in Greenville Robert renewed old friendships, and he and his wife Lucie took as active a part in the life of the community as his frequent trips across the country and the tedious room-by-room remodeling, from attic to basement, of the old Humber house would permit. Robert knew what changes he wanted to make in the house and how he wanted them made. Thus, he sought a carpenter whose work he liked and engaged him to work exclusively for him. This arrangement, which continued for many years, was convenient for Robert, whose workshop now was his home and whose life henceforth would be devoted to the public service of his fellow men.

When I asked Robert if he would like to become a member of the Greenville Rotary Club, I knew that an internationally minded person of his ideals would be thoroughly at home with the high ideals of an international service club such as Rotary. At that time, however, he was still continuing his grassroots campaign from state to state in behalf of world federation, and he was concerned about the number of local Rotary Club meetings he might have to miss. I explained that he could make up his local club meetings at any Rotary Club, anywhere in the world, and I added that, in a sense, he would be serving his local club and his community by making them known wherever he made up his meetings.

After his first month of Monday night meetings from 6:30 p.m. to 7:30 p.m. in the Greenville Rotary Building, I made it a point not to sit at the same table with Robert, because I knew that the things he wished to accomplish in his life were essentially political in nature, and I wanted him to have every opportunity to make as many new friends as possible. I never mentioned this fact to anyone, but somehow Robert knew what I was doing and soon, without any statement or verbal agreement, we began to meet in the foyer after the Rotary meeting. If neither of us had another engagement, we would walk out to my car or his car and talk for an hour or so.

Robert had a tendency to be long-winded, and so did I. One night we were sitting in the car in front of the Rotary Building talking, when a Greenville policeman arrived on his motorcycle. He stopped beside the car, recognized us, and exchanged greetings. As he turned to leave he asked, "Do you know what time it is?" We turned on our lights and learned to our surprise that it was 1:00 a.m. As he left we assumed that our conversation there at that hour of the night was disturbing someone in the neighborhood and of course we left.

Robert Lee Humber was a person of exceptional loyalty to his hometown and to his state, and he wanted the citizens of his state to have the privilege of enjoying the best that the civilized world could offer. In his travels and studies in Europe he was always looking for things and ideas which he thought could enrich the lives of the people back home.

During his early years as a student in Paris, he served as a tutor and a few times as a guide to the Louvre Museum. On one occasion he was selected as a guide to the Louvre for a group of American college and university presidents. When Robert was introduced to the group in the Louvre, the strong voice of one of the presidents in the midst of the group asked, "Who did you say our guide is?" Robert's name was repeated and out strode Dr. "Billy" Poteat, president of Wake Forest College to give his former student a big hug.

While living in Paris, Robert had become interested in art and had spent much time in its great museums. He felt that North Carolina, which boasted of many fine examples of interesting architecture, had neglected the field of art. After meeting and becoming well-acquainted with the American artist Louis Orr, whom France was celebrating as the world's greatest living etcher, Robert proposed that he "undertake to do the most outstanding work of his career on North Carolina: a series of fifty etchings plus a large-size State Capitol." Mr. Orr declined to consider the proposal at first but in June of 1939, less than three months before the declaration of war, he agreed to undertake Robert's commission. It is thus, thanks to the foresight, persuasiveness, and persistence of Robert Lee Humber and to Louis Orr for his magnanimous gift of twelve years of his life to North Carolina, that the North Carolina etchings became a reality, and North Carolinians of modest means became the primary beneficiaries of this great project.

Robert Lee Humber's love and concern for the people of North Carolina and his contagious belief in the future of the state also enabled him to inspire a second great gift of art to his state. He approached Mr. Samuel S. Kress with the unusual but challenging proposal that he, Robert Lee Humber, would attempt to persuade the members of the North Carolina General Assembly to allocate one million dollars for the purchase of works of art for the state, if Mr. Kress would agree to match that allocation with a gift of one million dollars' worth of art to be selected from his collection of Old Masters. Mr. Kress agreed but stipulated that his name not be revealed as the party offering to match the North Carolina Assembly's allocation.

Now, all Robert had to do was to persuade North Carolina politicians to do what no state assembly had ever dared do, i.e., vote to spend one million dollars of the taxpayers' money on works of art.

On April 10, 1951, Governor Kerr Scott sent the following special message to the North Carolina General Assembly:

> Never in North Carolina's history has such an opportunity been ours.
>
> A million dollars of outstanding Italian Renaissance art is now ours, if we act favorably. . . .
>
> This proposition permits North Carolina to receive not only a million dollars worth of Renaissance pictures, but cooperation with one of the wealthiest foundations in the world that will bring us through the years, without any cost to us, additional pictures and services of immense value.
>
> Such an offer is indeed rare. In our measured judgment, we simply cannot afford to reject it. In the one hundred and seventy-five years of our history, the state never has been able to establish a great art gallery; but it is now within our grasp. Any state of this union would not only welcome such an opportunity, but would also exert itself zealously to obtain it. Surely it would be unwise for us now to fumble the ball.
>
> This investment will be self-liquidating. Tourists, coming to visit our gallery, will reimburse this appropriation to North Carolina many times over a period of years. The ultimate cost to the

128

state will be absolutely negligible.

We earnestly request that no diversion of these funds be made to any project, however worthy. To destroy the constructive work of one state agency for the benefit of another is, in our opinion, a questionable method of attempting progress.

We urge, therefore, that the members of this General Assembly weigh seriously the advantages of this offer to the people of North Carolina. When opportunity knocks, it should be heeded. This is North Carolina's greatest hour in the field of art. Not only do we acquire art treasures of priceless value for the enjoyment of our people, but a source of endless inspiration to our children.

We approve House Bill 1086 and commend it to your favorable consideration subject to such amendments as the General Assembly may deem proper and expedient for the safeguarding of the funds.

House Bill 1086 was passed, and at Robert's request Governor Scott made arrangements for the old State Highway Building, which was being vacated at the time, to be used as a temporary museum for the display of the state's growing collection.

Robert Lee Humber was a self-disciplined, eye-minded person with an excellent power of concentration. He read profusely but selectively, and he remembered what he read. When young, he developed a habit of telling someone close to him what he had read or learned. In that manner, he put the new information in his own words and fixed it in his mind. Once there, it was his for life. Through his years of study at Wake Forest, Harvard, Oxford, and Paris, he became widely versed in many fields of learning and compiled an incredible store of knowledge in his memory.

Later in life, when asked to speak on a given subject, he seemed to need only to take a breath and start speaking. His thoughts on the subject would fall into place in an orderly manner as he spoke. His speeches were always well-documented, yet he always spoke extemporaneously. Such is the genius of a well-disciplined, well-documented, and well-developed human brain. Robert's reasoning processes were basically those of the historian. He learned or divined from the past the lessons he utilized to structure his theories of the future.

129

The great accomplishments of Robert Lee Humber were, I believe, essentially the result of great determination and effort on his part. His voice, according to his own evaluation, was too high-pitched for a good speaking voice. (Thus, while in Paris, he took voice lessons in an effort to develop his lower register.) A singer he was not. His vision was by far his greatest sensory asset, and he developed it to a very high degree. He learned to perceive in a glance not only the broad lines but the fine details, whose significance he then interpreted and recorded in his memory.

On a short bicycle trip with Robert to see the French countryside, I recall our getting a glimpse of an old church as we pedaled through a small village. As we came to smooth pavement on the opposite side of the little village, Robert said, "The church we just passed in the village is early Gothic. Its construction was probably begun during the first half of the twelfth century, but the details of its rosace and especially of its tower would seem to indicate that the villagers of that little community took more than one hundred years to complete its construction." Then he added, "If we returned and went into the crypt of that church, we might find heavy supporting Romanesque columns and arches. In that case, the time of beginning the construction could have been considerably earlier and the total time of constructing the church would have been even greater."

Robert's vision was very acute, and he was capable of great visual accuracy. One afternoon in Greenville, I accompanied him into the small front room of his father's house, where Mr. Congleton, the carpenter, was working. Robert's first words as he entered the room were, "Mr. Congleton, your molding line is not level." Mr. Congleton replied, "I measured it." Robert said, "Check it out." Mr. Congleton did and made a slight correction.

I was fascinated that afternoon as I watched Robert and Mr. Congleton creating a model of the molding for that room. The basic changes in the room had been completed. The beautiful walnut paneling was in place and the raised plaster circle in the ceiling was finished. Only a molding that would harmoniously unite the white ceiling and the walnut paneling was lacking. A single strip of molding around that room would have been hopelessly insignificant. It was obvious that a suitable molding would have to be created by the skillful blending of a number of pieces of molding. Robert had already visualized the molding he wanted in that room. He was fully aware that the addition of each piece of molding would require slow, painstaking study, during which he would have to keep in mind the other pieces to be added. Mr. Congleton was apparently endowed with the patience needed to give Robert ample time to select each piece of molding and let him explain how he wanted it joined to the others. Sometimes he had to tear it out and try again, until the final piece of molding was in place.

I did not remain that afternoon until the model was completed, but I saw it later. The model, approximately two and one-half feet long, consisted of eleven assembled pieces of molding. When the molding for that room was finally put in place, it not only accomplished its purpose of uniting the white ceiling and walnut paneling, it established a dignity of setting for the handsome Baccarat glass chandelier suspended from the center of the raised plaster circle of the ceiling.

In the south wall of that room, in line with the chandelier, was an open fireplace, framed in a sturdy Italian mantelpiece of white marble. On the mantle Robert later placed two magnificent bronze busts: one of George Washington on the left and one of Benjamin Franklin on the right.

Built along the wall to the right and left of the fireplace were large matching display cabinets designed somewhat like wide Romanesque doorways. The decorative trim of the cabinets, fitting against the paneling, concealed the fact that the cabinets in the wall were actually on rollers and indeed at times did serve as doors to hidden closets behind them. When that room was finished and handsomely furnished, it became my favorite room in the house.

Incidentally, before going to bed at night, or perhaps to avoid going to bed so early, Robert's boys, when young, loved for him to go with them to that room to give George and Ben a pat on the head and say, "Good night, George, Good night, Ben. " I am sure that Robert, the historian, took advantage of those cherished moments to tell the boys a few stories about George and Ben.

Robert Lee Humber was a person whose daily three-block walk to mailbox no. 75 in the old post office building at the corner of Evans and Third streets was not the short ten-minute walk it could have been. When he left home each morning around 10:00 a.m., his wife, Lucie, was certain only that she could count on his being back home in time for lunch. He greeted everybody along the way and often stopped to talk. Within a few weeks of settling in, he knew all the merchants, something about their businesses, and most of the clerks in the downtown area.

This daily routine, which he took over to relieve his father soon after he returned to America, served him well some years later when he was gathering statistics to be used in his application for a technical institute for Pitt County. Having been born and reared in Greenville, he was fully aware that there were many people in the area who needed only the opportunity of developing an appropriate skill in order to raise their standard of living and he wanted them to have that opportunity.

In the hope of locating a capable person who might be interested in accepting the challenge of seeking a technical institute for Pitt County, Robert communicated with a number of educators in Pitt County. Most favored the idea but were too busy to do anything about it.

Robert remembered the story of his grandfather's stroke in 1878, which forced his father to take over his woodworking and blacksmith shop in an attempt to earn a living for his mother and his three sisters at a time when there was no technical institute around to give him advice. In the late 1950s, Robert Lee Humber became determined not to let the opportunity of establishing a technical institute in Pitt County die because of lack of interest. When there were only three unassigned openings for technical institutes in North Carolina remaining, Robert set out on foot, going from merchant to merchant in the downtown area of Greenville, gathering statistics which he felt would be required for any serious application. I saw him set out alone that first morning, but I no longer remember how long he continued to pound the pavement of Greenville and neighboring communities before he was joined by enough persons of like mind to guarantee adequate evidence of need and assurance of success to draft his application. I know only that with the cooperation and help of many businesses, industries and friends, he was finally able in 1961 to submit a winning application. I had never seen that document until August 17, 1987, when I received a copy which I requested in order to confirm the accuracy of my memory. The following paragraphs taken from the latter part of Robert's application for a technical school for Pitt County will give some idea of the thoroughness of his survey and of

132

the extent to which the county as a whole became a part of it:

Referring specifically to the criteria, the following data are submitted:

1. Evidence of Need as shown by the Survey. A census of existing skilled employment in Pitt County has been conducted: 156 individual firms have reported that at least 161 classifications of skilled labor now exist in Pitt County; that 2,204 persons are employed in these industries; that 497 positions are now waiting to be filled; that during the next 12 months 1,184 new positions or replacements can be expected; and that 1,307 persons are now desirous of improving their competence by pursuing courses in the actual fields of their employment.

2. Evidence of Financial Support. In addition to providing a site of twenty-five acres for the Industrial Center, the County Board of Commissioners is prepared to submit a bond issue of $300,000.00 to provide suitable buildings for a Technical School in Pitt County that would be constructed according to the specifications prescribed by the State Board of Education. Interpreting the opinion of citizens throughout our County, an overwhelming approval of the bond issue may be expected.

3. Evidence of Endorsement on the part of Existing Industry. Not only does the enclosed Survey indicate the interest of Existing Industry in support of the curricula offered in the Technical School, but the accompanying letters testify to the widespread and enthusiastic support of this project in Pitt County.

The said letters come from the following organizations, firms, and individuals:

1. Pitt County Board of Education, a certified copy of excerpts from Minutes of the Pitt County Board of Education Meeting on November 7, 1960.
2. Superintendent of Pitt County Schools
3. Superintendent of Greenville City Schools
4. Principal, Farmville Public Schools
5. Principal, Ayden Public Schools
6-17. Chairmen of the twelve School Districts of Pitt County
18. Mayor of Greenville
19. Mayor of Farmville
20. Mayor of Ayden
21. Mayor of Grifton

22. Mayor of Bethel
23. City Manager of Greenville and Superintendent of Greenville Utilities Company
24. City Manager of Ayden
25. Pitt County Development Commission
26. Director, Pitt County Development Commission
27. Director, Farmville Economic Council
28. Greenville Chamber of Commerce
29. Farmville Chamber of Commerce
30. Ayden Chamber of Commerce
31. Greenville Junior Chamber of Commerce
32. Ayden Junior Chamber of Commerce
33. President, East Carolina College
34. Voice of America - see Survey
35. E.I. duPont de Nemours and Company
36. Union Carbide Consumer Products Company, Greenville Division
37. Formica Corporation
38. Carolina Telephone and Telegraph Company
39. North State Garment Company, Farmville
40. WNCT TV, Channel 9
41. Carolina Dairies
42. Jenkins Motor Company
43. Daily Reflector - Greenville newspaper
44. Blount Fertilizer and Allied Industries
45. Wachovia Bank and Trust Company, Greenville
46. State Bank and Trust Company, Greenville
47. Planters National Bank and Trust Company, Greenville
48. Official opinion of the Department of Justice of North Carolina that Pitt County is authorized to issue county-wide school bonds and is not restricted to district school bonds.
49-56. Brochures dealing with different aspects of Pitt County - its economic, industrial, social, and educational life, that were prepared by the Pitt County Development Commission for the purpose of informing prospective industries regarding conditions now prevailing in the County.

In conversing with the managers of the different industrial plants operating in our County, such as Formica, Union Carbide, Voice of America, Fieldcrest, Carolina Telephone and Telegraph Company, the various tobacco industries, and automotive companies, as the enclosed letters will reveal, they declared that the most difficult problem facing the management of these organizations is obtaining skilled labor. At the present time many of these firms are seeking trained personnel outside of North Carolina.

This deficiency in our economic life cannot be overemphasized. The need for a Technical School in Pitt County is incontestable; the growing mechanization of agriculture, including the cultivation of tobacco, accentuates it. More farm labor each year will be unemployed. This labor should be taught trades and provided employment at home. Otherwise, both the local community and the State will lose invaluable economic and human resources annually.

Confirming the necessity of a reservoir of skilled labor as indispensable to inducing industries to locate in our County, I can cite my recent experience in New York, when the owner of one of the most important manufacturers of stapling machines in America informed me, after numerous conferences, that he would be prepared to establish a plant in Pitt County, subject to his verification of the labor situation in our area. He had already manifested his friendship for our State by the presentation of over $100,000.00 in gifts to the North Carolina State Art Society. During a subsequent visit on my part to New York, he informed me that he would be unable to fulfill his intentions, since, upon investigation, he had found that Pitt County did not have either a supply of skilled labor, or a school which could permit workmen to be specifically trained to produce his product.

If Eastern North Carolina is ever to grow into an important industrial area, Technical Schools will have to be established to supply the personnel required for incoming industry.

When the time came to start planning the buildings Robert recommended the classical facade with pediment and columns which he felt would give the buildings the beauty and dignity they would need.

Chapter XIII

When Robert told me he was planning to run for the office of North Carolina state senator from Pitt County, I was not surprised; and when he announced his candidacy on Thursday, February 27, 1958, I informed my cousin Dr. Paul Jones, the incumbent, that this time I expected to support my friend Robert Lee Humber. Paul, who had already held the office approximately nine years, was not particularly pleased with my decision, but later, on March 21, 1958, he graciously announced that he would not seek re-election, adding: "There are many capable and outstanding citizens of Pitt County who should be called upon to serve in the General Assembly. Two of such outstanding citizens have already announced publicly their desire to serve in the Senate at the next session, and others have expressed an interest in becoming candidates. I feel that this is as it should be and is conducive to good government."

Earlier, when J. Henry Harrell entered the race, I had been forced to reassess Robert's chances and, frankly, the more I learned, the less certain I was that Robert could win.

It is true that Robert Lee Humber had been a Democrat all his life, but so had his opponent, J. Henry Harrell. Moreover, Mr. Harrell, who had moved from Bertie to Pitt County, had married Rosa Lee Lang, a member of a well-known Farmville family, and had settled in Greenville. Robert Lee Humber, on the other hand, though born in Greenville, had been away from Pitt County, except for rare, transient visits, since he first went to college in 1914, and he did not return to settle down in Greenville until Hitler's invasion forced him to leave France in 1940. That was twenty-six years, a whole generation, that he was away from Pitt County.

How many people born in Pitt County during that generation would know Robert Lee Humber, who, incidentally, spent five more years, after returning home, traveling across the nation in behalf of world federation? And how many of those Pitt County natives, now of voting age, would Robert recognize?

Furthermore, during the last ten years before Robert returned to America, his opponent, J. Henry Harrell, a successful attorney and father of a fine family, had practiced law in Greenville, the county seat, and simultaneously operated several farms in Pitt County, which was basically an agricultural county. Mr. Harrell was not only a Democrat of long standing; he was an active member of the local party organization and had served as chairman of the Pitt County Board of Elections for fifteen years. Many of the "regular" Democrats felt that Henry had earned the right to party support and that it was "his turn" to go to the state senate if that was what he wanted to do. Robert, on the other hand, had never even hung out his shingle to practice law in Pitt County, and he was definitely not a farmer.

About the time that Mr. Harrell was beginning his law practice in Greenville, Robert was offered an exceptional business opportunity in Paris. The president of an American oil firm asked Robert Lee Humber to organize the European investment branch of his firm in Paris and to serve as its executive director and its legal counselor. He also accepted Robert's remuneration proposal which permitted Robert to invest substantially in the company's operations.

Since I was in Paris when the proposal was made and also there again during the last three years before the debacle, I was aware of Robert's success. Sitting in his office one day in 1938, discussing the effect of the war of nerves on business, Robert commented that any man willing to apply himself to the task could become a millionaire. As usual, that day we talked too long, and Robert, being pressed to catch a commuter train, handed me a $5,000 bill to deposit for him. His customers were of many nationalities and, of course, the currency varied but not necessarily according to nationality. In 1940, after working ten years in the world of international business and finance, Robert was financially able to return to Greenville and devote the remainder of his life to the public service of his fellowmen. That fact, in itself, was difficult for struggling Pitt County farmers and laborers to understand.

The fact that Robert Lee Humber, the scholar, was adept at handling money probably did not surprise old Greenville residents, who still remembered the often-told story of the business acumen of his father, a physically strong but gentle man. According to the version of that story which I heard, Mr. "Billy" Woolard, president of the Greenville Bank and Trust Company on Evans Street, rushed into Mr. Humber's machine shop on Fifth Street one morning and asked Mr. Humber to come with him to the bank to unlock the safe. Mr.

Woolard had opened the bank and the customers were there, but he had not been able to open the safe.

After about ten minutes, Mr. Humber had the safe open and a smiling Mr. Woolard asked, "How much will that be, Mr. Humber?"

In his habitual manner of responding to that question, Mr. Humber put his hands in his pockets, looked thoughtfully toward the ceiling, then replied, "That will be $25.00."

Mr. Woolard's smile vanished as he exclaimed, "$25.00 for ten minutes' work! I won't pay it."

Mr. Humber calmly closed the safe door and turned to leave. Mr. Woolard, following closely behind, protested, "You can't do that. We've got to use that safe to do business." Mr. Humber was nearing the front entrance of the bank when Mr. Woolard stopped him saying, "Go back and open it, Mr. Humber, we'll pay what you ask."

It took Mr. Humber a little longer the second time, but when the lock bolt clicked and the door opened, Mr. Woolard was standing close by. With a forced smile on his face, he asked, "And what did you say that would be, Mr. Humber?" Mr. Humber replied, "You must remember, Billy, that you are paying not merely for my time, but for my knowledge." Then Mr. Humber put his hands in his pockets, looked thoughtfully toward the ceiling, and hesitating only long enough to pucker his lips and whistle one short note, he turned and said, "That will be $50.00."

I am certain that Robert Lee Humber, whose beautifully paneled and handsomely appointed offices occupying the entire top floor of 44 Avenue des Champs Elysées in Paris, possessed far greater knowledge of the business and financial world than did his father, but I doubt that his profit percentage was any greater!

Robert Lee Humber was a gentleman of impeccable character, always inspired by noble ideals. His magnificent accomplishments, some of which were already beginning to enrich the lives of his fellowmen, were not designed, however, to corral votes for him in a Pitt County election. His long and successful effort to persuade Louis Orr, the most renowned etcher of our time, to give twelve years of his life to the state of North Carolina would bring few votes to Robert Lee Humber. His greatest and most noble effort in behalf of world peace through world federation was recognized across the nation and beyond as a superb and potentially great contribution to the future welfare of mankind, but how many people in Pitt County would vote to send Robert Lee Humber to the North Carolina Senate because he was interested in world peace? His successful effort to obtain one million dollars' worth of famous Renaissance art for North Carolina from Mr. Samuel S. Kress would probably cost him votes. How many Pitt County voters would favor spending one million dollars of the taxpayers' money for the purchase of art?

The day that Mr. Harrell announced his candidacy and the political campaign got under way, all I could picture in my mind was Henry Harrell, on the inside track supported by the "machine," with his pockets figuratively already stuffed with rural votes. I felt that Robert could count on some support from the college community, and I knew that he would receive votes from old Greenville residents, but I did not know where the necessary drive and enthusiasm to get out that vote would come from until Robert approached a small group of young Greenville businessmen who knew and admired him and were happy to see a man of his calibre enter the race.

I was not present at their first meeting, but I was told by one of those present that when Robert stated that he was planning to run for the office of state senator from Pitt County, their first question was, "What kind of an organization do you have?" With a warm smile expressing complete confidence in them, Robert replied, "You are my organization."

To imagine their reaction to Robert's statement, it is necessary to know who was present at that meeting. In a sense, they were the vigorous young voice of old Greenville—the very ones who could awaken old Greenville residents and get out the vote which was there for Robert Lee Humber. There were five of them present at that first meeting with Robert:

1. *Charles O'Hagan Horne, Jr.*, son of "Doc" Horne, the pharmacist, whose drugstore was a popular gathering place on Evans Street next door to the old *Daily Reflector* office, which was located for many years at the corner of Evans and Third streets. Charles was a local electrical contractor and engineer who, during the political campaign, on March 7, 1958, was named to a five-year term on the Greenville Utilities Commission to replace Reynolds May. Charles became the political analyst and manager of Robert Lee Humber's campaign.

2. *David Jordan Whichard II*, named for his grandfather who, as owner and editor of *The Daily Reflector* awakened "the dirty little town on the Tar" at the turn of the century and started it on a course of enlightened progress into this century. The elder Whichard and Professor W. H. Ragsdale were loyal friends of my father, who in 1907 was struggling to win passage of his bill to establish East Carolina Teachers Training School (today E.C.U.). Dave's father, David Julian Whichard, then a twelve-year-old page in the House of Representatives, was also working for the passage of that bill.

During the session young Dave befriended and gathered under his wing two younger pages whose fathers were representatives from the western part of the state. When the time came to vote on the bill, young Dave was in a position to persuade the two western representatives to vote with the east. David Jordan Whichard II, a former president of the Jaycees, was, in 1958, an editor on the staff of *The Daily Reflector.*

3. *J. B. Kittrell, Jr.*, son of the very popular charter member of the Greenville Rotary Club (1919) and the former Elizabeth Hinton, my high school history teacher, had just completed a stint as treasurer of the Junior Chamber of Commerce and had joined his father's firm of J. B. Kittrell, Sugar Brokers, Inc.

4. *John Lautares*, whose father John and his Uncle Pete Lautares were owners and operators of Greenville's first Candy Kitchen, was a popular star athlete on the Greenville High School's State Championship Basketball Team of the late 1930s. The Candy Kitchen, located on Evans Street just two doors from Five Points was at that time John's hangout and the gathering place of the younger generation, which included many college students and some ladies and gentlemen of an older generation who just couldn't resist those delicious ice cream sundaes and banana splits. The ladies seemed to eat theirs slowly in order to enjoy the delectable taste of each morsel. Occasionally, however, a hefty, athletic gourmand would come in, order a banana split, gulp it down with gluttonous glee, and then try to find someone who would bet him that he couldn't eat another one. In 1958, John, following the example of his older brother George, had become owner and operator of a jewelry business on Fifth Street.

5. *W. M. (Booger) Scales, Jr.*, who had just been named on January 24, 1958, "The Outstanding Man of the Year" by the Junior Chamber of Commerce, was full of pep and raring to go. His first words to Robert, I am told, were "you are the horse and the race is on," and henceforth he addressed Robert Lee Humber as "Horse." Booger was a free spirit who added the kick of horseplay to the campaign and a vocabulary in which he knew that the serious intellectually inclined Robert Lee Humber would be woefully deficient. Thus the race and the fun began.

Since my duties at East Carolina College made it difficult for me to attend frequent meetings, it was suggested at the second meeting that I take responsibility for getting out the college vote. The underlying assumption seemed to suggest that a majority of the college vote would go to the scholar, Robert Lee Humber, and therefore the greater the college vote, the greater Robert Lee Humber's chance of winning the election.

After pondering my assignment, I began to doubt the validity of that assumption. I reasoned that, if all the faculty members on campus were as broadly educated as was Robert Lee Humber, the assumption might be valid. But some college professors earn degrees which lead to specialization rather than to broad education. A few professors even tend to belittle the value of a broad education, calling such studies "a waste of the students' time." Moreover, the election included the entire college community. Thus I could not be certain that merely getting out the vote of the college community would necessarily enhance Robert Lee Humber's chance of winning the election.

I therefore tried to stir some interest in Robert Humber and his campaign on campus. In order to do that without awakening the opposition, I resorted to speaking individually to friends on campus who, I felt, would prefer Robert over his opponent. If the reaction was favorable, I related some interesting aspects of Robert's college and university experiences, gave briefly his family background, and mentioned some of his accomplishments. Then I expressed the opinion that Robert's success in the Pitt County election could very well depend upon the support he received from the college community. Incidentally, one of the best advocates of Robert Humber on campus was not a member of the faculty or the administration. It was Mr. McArthur, a member of the campus staff.

I continued this individual approach until the second week in May, when I stopped to prepare a leaflet inviting the college community to join the citizens of Greenville in the upcoming Pitt County election. I have been unable to find a copy of that leaflet, but I recall that it consisted principally of a map of Greenville delineating the wards, locating the voting places, and giving information on registration and voting procedures. I signed the leaflet so that those who wished further information would get in touch with me.

I missed the next meeting which, I believe, was held in the office of Dr. Henry Aldridge. I understand that it was a long but constructive session which ended rather abruptly.

It appears that late in the meeting one member of the group became inspired to render a stirring eulogy of our candidate. He praised him as a gentleman and a scholar and as an outstanding linguist whose vast vocabulary included not only a few of our distinctively Southern expressions, but also the intellectual vocabulary and wisdom of Harvard Yard, Oxford University, and even the Sorbonne. "But," said the speaker, "Horse, since you became our candidate, I have been doing a little research in the demographic metalinguistics of Pitt County, and I have found a stratum of human society which I fear you will be unable to reach and we need those votes."

Then, shifting his tongue to the other cheek, he delivered a devastating challenge to our gentlemanly candidate. "I am thinking," he said, "of the dropout, the jobless, the downtrodden, the drunk, and yes, the local vocal yokel, the superb hog-caller, who thinks he can sing beautiful country music. Those poor devils can't speak or even understand your language. To get their votes you must speak to them in their vernacular. Their vocabulary is not large, so, in order to help you, Horse, I have prepared a short list of key words used repeatedly by them, which I think you should know." Then with an impish twinkle in his eye, he said, "They are. . . ."

Thanks to the sudden boisterous outburst of laughter following the first word, the speaker's voice was drowned out and the meeting came to a hilarious end. And thus it was that our distinguished candidate was rescued from the embarrassment of becoming the first Rhodes scholar to completely fail a vocabulary test of selected short words, none exceeding four letters in length.

About a week later, Robert asked me to take some posters out the road to Bethel and place them in store windows. On leaving Bethel after completing the job, I noticed that one of the first posters I had been given permission to place in a show window had already been removed. As I approached the House Station area on my way back to Greenville, I saw a big black Cadillac sedan parked on the shoulder of the road. A man, neatly dressed in a conservative dark blue suit, white shirt, dark tie and black shoes was standing in a field nearby talking to two laborers. It was Robert Lee Humber politicking.

That night I drove to Robert's house, handed him my car keys, and told him that my Chevrolet could go places in the country that his Cadillac couldn't go. Then I suggested that he drive his Cadillac in the backyard and close the gate until after the primary.

Meanwhile, the original group of five were calling on their friends and spreading their political influence throughout Greenville and into the neighboring communities of Pitt County. Charles Horne was coordinating the efforts being made and drafting detailed plans for the work to be carried out during the last two weeks of the campaign. His notes, which I have read, reveal the names of approximately two hundred volunteers to whom he assigned work which they could do and wanted to do. There was a large group of women who preferred to serve in making telephone calls. Some volunteers could work better out in the county or in the communities where they lived, and a number of volunteers were assigned specific tasks to be carried out on election day.

In harmony with Robert's desire that nothing derogatory be said about his opponent, newspaper advertisements were prepared concentrating entirely on Robert Lee Humber, his accomplishments, and qualifications.

During the campaign, I spoke to a member of the League of Women Voters with reference to sponsoring a television program presenting both senatorial candidates to the people of Pitt County, and I learned that many of Robert's fans had already spoken to her on that subject. In any case, the League of Women Voters rendered a valuable service to the people of Pitt County, who were given an excellent opportunity to see, hear, and compare the two candidates.

As the campaign drew to a close, the excitement was running high, because it had become obvious that Robert Humber was gaining ground and gradually diminishing the great advantage that Mr. Harrell held at the start with local party organization support.

On election day, John Lautares stopped me and asked, "Who do you think I just saw?"

"I don't know. Who?"

"Jack Spain."

"What did Jack have to say?"

"He didn't say anything. I did all the talking."

After taking out a cigarette, placing it in his cigarette-holder and lighting up, he assumed his typical FDR cigarette pose and continued, "I told him to turn right around, go back to Washington, and tell his congressman that we sent him to Washington to represent us, not to send someone down to Pitt County to tell us how to vote."

With that said, John thumped his cigarette-holder and watched the first light ashes as they drifted to the ground.

That evening a large crowd gathered in the blocked-off section of Cotanche Street in front of *The Daily Reflector* building to watch the returns as they were posted.

Early in the evening as the rural votes came in, Mr. Harrell took a big lead which did not narrow until the Greenville vote had been posted.

Late in the evening, with Mr. Harrell still holding the lead and only a few boxes remaining to be heard from, a lady who had never taken an active part in politics before rushed up to Robert and asked, "If the remaining boxes don't put us out in front, what are we going to do?"

Robert smiled and replied, "We are going to congratulate the opponent."

"Oh!" she said.

A few minutes later Booger Scales, who had been upstairs in the recording room and back down in the street numerous times during the evening, approached Robert and said, "Horse, if Bill Stroud comes in with enough votes from Ayden to put us over the hump, so help me, I'm going to give you a big kiss, right there." Robert replied, "I think we can also count on Mrs. Spencer of Black Jack to help us over the top."

About thirty minutes later Mrs. Spencer, followed closely by Bill Stroud, went upstairs to the *Reflector* recording room. Everything got quiet upstairs and down in the street below, because these boxes would determine the winner. From where we were standing in the street, we could see the heads of those in charge of tabulating the results. As the counting got underway we noticed a few persons rushing back and forth as if checking the figures and making comparisons, and we could sense the excitement building in that room. Suddenly we heard Mrs. Spencer shout, "We've beat the machine. We've beat the machine." The first person to come running down the stairs and straight to Robert was Booger, pretending he was going to carry out his threat, but instead he gave Robert a big hug and congratulations.

The final talley was Harrell, 4599; Humber, 4833.

Although Robert Lee Humber had many old friends he could count on, I do not believe that Robert could have won the election without the loyalty and hard work of his chosen team of the five young Greenville businessmen and their numerous friends.

Chapter XIV

During his years of speaking in behalf of world federation and dealing with legislators in states across the nation, followed by more years of working with North Carolina legislators on various projects, Robert Lee Humber had gained an invaluable background rarely enjoyed by a freshman senator. When he took his seat in the North Carolina Senate, he was already well-known in political circles. He enjoyed the challenge which the senate presented and, as always, he was an indefatigable worker. His interests were broad. In fact, Robert was probably equally well prepared to serve in the United States Senate, but what he now wanted to accomplish in the North Carolina Senate was to raise the standard of living and the quality of life of North Carolinians. He understood that this could be done most effectively through education.

He therefore strove to improve education and to increase educational opportunities at all levels for North Carolina citizens. He introduced "a bill to promote and encourage education beyond the high school level in North Carolina," "a bill to appropriate funds to the State Board of Education for the purpose of establishing and equipping community colleges," and "a bill to encourage attendance in institutions of higher learning by providing a scholar incentive program for residents of North Carolina." He cosponsored, with Senators White and Walton, "a bill to establish in North Carolina a school for professional training in music and other performing arts for the Southern region," and with eight other senators he cosponsored "a bill to provide scholarship funds for graduate nurses who complete courses in accredited schools in the field of anesthesia." Finally, he introduced "a bill to establish annual awards for outstanding achievements by citizens of North Carolina." Incidentally, some years later, he was named the recipient of the North Carolina Award for Public

Service.

One of his most gratifying accomplishments in the North Carolina Senate was the completion of the project he had initiated in Greenville leading to the establishment of Pitt Technical Institute, which he later guided to the status of Pitt Community College. Here is a letter he received upon the completion of that task:

North Carolina
State Board of Education
A.C. Davis, Controller
306 Education Building
Raleigh

Asheboro, North Carolina
June 22, 1961

Honorable Robert Lee Humber
Greenville
North Carolina

Dear Mr. Humber :

I read with a great deal of interest the account of your successful bond election in Pitt County. The favorable majority vote was impressive and shows that a lot of effort was put forth in presenting the industrial education program to the people. As in every case when people are properly informed, they will support this program which can mean so much to the future of our state.

Your own leadership in securing approval of the State Board of Education and the General Assembly made the program possible for the county, and your people should be eternally grateful to you for your dedicated service in this and many other matters.

Congratulations on a job well done!

Sincerely,

Charles W. McCrary, Chairman
Vocational Committee
State Board of Education

CWM:ia
cc: Mr. A. Wade Martin

Robert Humber's belief that North Carolina was historically well-represented in architecture but lacking in the field of art led to his years of search for ways to correct that deficiency. It led him to the world's greatest etcher of our time, Louis Orr, whom he was finally able to persuade to give twelve years of his life to the state of North Carolina producing his now famous North Carolina Etchings. It led him to ask Mr. Samuel S. Kress if he would give a million dollars' worth of his famous Renaissance art collection to the state of North Carolina if he, Robert Lee Humber, would persuade the North Carolina General Assembly to match that gift by allocating one million dollars for the purchase of additional art for the state.

In acquiring Orr's etchings and amassing art from the Kress collection to be displayed in the capital city of North Carolina, Robert Lee Humber was obviously establishing a commanding, visible need for a great art museum to house the state's growing art treasures.

On November 9, 1970, in commemoration of the twenty-fifth anniversary of the founding of the United Nations, Robert Lee Humber addressed his fellow Rotarians in the Greenville, North Carolina Rotary Building, which they had constructed in 1920. Speaking extemporaneously as usual, Robert Lee Humber delivered the following address:

> Fellow Rotarians, this evening will you permit me to preface my remarks by the comment that our age marks a great transitional epoch in human history. It is comparable to other epochs that have characterized the development of Western Culture. I would think, in terms of comparison, with what Western Culture con- fronted, when the Roman empire came into existence and consolidated many kingdoms under the rule of law, extending its sovereignty over Europe. I am thinking, that was a definitive effort representing the common aspirations and the mutual endeavors of the people living at that time. They had a common goal.
>
> Following that came the Middle Ages, and that great epoch left us a magnificent legacy. We don't think about it often, but we are speaking this evening in the English language. There is also a French language, a Spanish, and an Italian, all developed in the Middle Ages. We go to universities the Middle Ages organized, the faculties of these institutions the same as we have today. They built

cathedrals that pierced the very skyline of heaven. It was the age of faith. The Middle Ages through several centuries combined and motivated the different aspirations of our forebears.

Then it was succeeded by another epoch, the Renaissance. And the Renaissance said: "Man is the Measure of all things. (Let him) climb out on the noonday meridian of his potential. Let him accomplish anything, dare anything." And so it gave us Columbus; it gave us Galileo; it gave us Shakespeare. All of these names, added to certain others like Raphael, Michelangelo, Leonardo da Vinci, they sound like the Te Deum in a cathedral choir, a magnificent heritage for us all.

Then came another epoch when human energies were concentrated in one supreme effort for reformation, trying to recapture some of the lost titles of the religious freedom that our forebears experienced and under, not only Martin Luther, but Calvin, Zwingli, Knox, they forged a tremendous legacy for us today.

And then, the energies of men focused on another objective, the Industrial Revolution. For two hundred years, that Revolution had been active. Up to that time, about eighty-five percent of the people worked in order to keep fifteen percent in a state of reason-able convenience in living habits of conduct. And the masses said: "We must participate; we are not prepared to remain indefinitely among the eighty-five; we are going to join the fifteen." So they resorted to the machine, and the machine began to fabricate this wealth, began to distribute it, and the standards of living of the individual began to rise. And that process is still in progress.

We are living at this hour at another great transition epoch of human history. I think it is comparable to the epoch of the Eighteenth Century, when Feudalism was summoned to validate its continuance as the regime of human government. Contemplate six or seven hundred years of active governmental authority and then this regime being summoned to justify its continuation. Many times in Paris I have stood on the Rue de Rivoli, looking across to the Tuileries Gardens. There is the plaque indicating the site of the Old National Assembly when Feudalism was abolished. I can hear the words of men like Gregoire and others in that Convention, "Don't abolish Feudalism. I was born under it, my father was, my grandfathers, and on for generations. We can't abolish that!" But Feudalism had reached the apogee of its capacity to give to the individual protection for his property and the continued possession and defense of his rights. And so, a new transition at that time was negotiated, and nationalism just burst forth at the very seams of society, populating all the areas of the earth, creating a power that survives today in many, retrospectively, in many areas of the globe.

And today we are facing another great transition in human history, and that transition marks something unprecedented. We are beginning at the very dawn of the Nuclear Age. The Nuclear Age, due to scientific progress, has united the world by transportation, communication of ideas, creating a solidarity of economic interest. They are beginning to speak as the individual feels, "I'm a citizen of this planet and how are we going to order the planet, and what are we going to do to preserve the heritage that we have received?" That is the greatest and the foremost issue, I believe, before our generation. What is it that you and I can do? What *is* at stake?

I mentioned the Industrial Revolution a moment ago and then followed by the Nuclear Revolution now in progress. Sometime ago, when I had the pleasure of speaking to the chairman of the Nuclear Fission Committee of the University of Chicago, I reminded him of an essay I had read by the former president of MIT. And he said: "Compare the Industrial Revolution in its mechanical development with the Nuclear Revolution of today." How would you compare it? Take two pounds of coal, put them in a stove. Those two pounds of coal will irradiate eight kilowatt hours of energy. But if you put those two pounds of coal through the Atomic processes of extracting their properties, you don't get eight kilowatt hours of energy, but twenty-five *billion* kilowatt hours of energy. The Nuclear Age that is dawning!

I know that there are people living today who are quite content to say: "The old regime was satisfactory to me. I have no desire either to change it or even to adjust myself to something new!" But we cannot reject the inevitable. We can't secede from this globe. We can't destroy geography. Incumbent upon us is to try to analyze what is necessary for the security of our civilization. We build cities, we establish hospitals, and we all are proud of what occurred in our community last Tuesday.[1] We build institutions for the education of the masses; then with a flash—in the 59 seconds that it took over Hiroshim—one

---

[1]The Hospital Bond Issue was passed by the voters.

hundred twenty thousand human beings were pulverized, their bodies carbonized.

What is the foremost issue of our Day? May I suggest to you, it is the security of our heritage. And if we attempt to perpetuate on the old principles what we have received, we may be in a serious dilemma. As we look back, each of these epochs that I have just mentioned, alluded to, rather, each of these represents a consolidated effort on the part of the generations of that time to reach a certain goal. Religious freedom, yes! Solidarity in economic development for the masses, yes! But our generation today has no precedent to guide it; we are a global community. We send men to the moon and we neglect, if we don't completely ignore, the solutions of the problems here on earth. This is our foremost preoccupation.

What is it that can guide us today? Throughout history there have been efforts made to reconcile the conflicting interests of nations. These efforts have followed invariably a certain characteristic. They have embodied a certain approach: how to achieve peace between these communities, recognized at different epochs to be sovereign. And we have christened that approach under the name of diplomacy; and whether we are dealing with a Delion League, or a Peloponnesian League, or the Hanseatic League, or the Articles of Confederation, the League of Nations, or the United Nations, the one outstanding principle has been diplomacy.

And what is diplomacy? Diplomacy is nothing but the voluntary cooperation of nations. Voluntarius, I stress the word voluntary, because there is no binding commitment under diplomacy that is enforceable in courts. Let us, for example, just allude to the League of Nations, founded in 1919. It came forward with the maximum authority that it could, but it didn't have enough authority. Next, in 1935 came Mussolini going down into Abyssinia, and the League said to Mussolini: "Get out. You even had sponsored the presentation of the country of Abyssinia as a member of the League of Nations, and now you are violating its integrity. Get Out." Following the precedent of Japan going into Manchuria, Mussolini got out of the League. And then finally in 1939, came the invasion of Poland.

The crisis of diplomacy is realistic. Let's don't deceive ourselves that we are relying on a broken reed. Diplomacy has never been able to preserve peace at a moment of crisis. Now, diplomacy accomplishes a great deal; but after World War II, we inaugurated another diplomatic order.

The only reason why we have the United Nations instead of the continuation of the League of Nations, of course, is the fact that the League of Nations expelled Russia when it invaded Finland and it would not come back into the League. And Roosevelt did not want to resurrect the controversy in America whether it should join in an international diplomatic order. So they rechristened it "United Nations," the only additional serious feature being the trusteeship.

Now, the United Nations is here. Has it accomplished its mission? Let me speak first of all of the humanitarian aspects of the United Nations. They are magnificent accomplishments. It would be difficult to exaggerate what the institution has done for countries throughout the world. When you think, the population of our globe today is around three billion four hundred and eighty million - half of the human race tonight goes to bed hungry, twenty percent of the human race can't read or write, ninety percent of certain countries are completely illiterate. The United Nations has gone in to establish fellowships, trying to bring the adults of these countries to other countries where they can be disciplined, informed and equipped to go back home to establish schools. A magnificent service! They have taken in the able-bodied people of these regions, given them technical instruction, going back to establish highways, hospitals; in other words, vitalizing those areas of human interest that need to be mobilized for human progress and equipped with intelligent leadership. Without the U.N., that would not have been accomplished.

The criticism is not of the humanitarian aspects of the United Nations' achievements; they have gone into all areas of the world. In terms of malaria, they have vaccinated over three hundred million children. Tremendous! And hundreds of thousands die annually *now* from preventable diseases; hundreds of millions are crippled. The U.N. hasn't finished its functions; it has accepted the assignments and is moving ahead. In terms of the world bank: the credit that has been extended to local countries, attempting to enable them to improve their local conditions instead of being the recipients of the benefactions of other countries! And whether you go into this area or that area, the humanitarian aspects of the U.N. has given it a validity, justified its creation. And without the U.N. today, there wouldn't be any international forum where a nation's aspirations could be presented, respected and, if possible, implemented by the cooperative efforts of all nations, that are members of the U.N.

151

When the U.N. was formed back in 1945, fifty nations gathered in San Francisco. I recall, with very vivid memories, the two months that they were in progress. The leaders of the fifty nations gathered there, disposed to try to eradicate the tragedy of war. Today there are one hundred and twenty-six nations, members of the U.N. Over eight hundred million people on this globe now have received the status of a full-fledged citizenship, emerging from colonialism due to the efforts of the U.N. You and I, perhaps, can't quite appreciate what it means to a man, we'll say, living over there, somewhere in Mesopotamia, when he says: "I have no education, I can't read, no hospital around, not even a road; but somehow something's happening around here and my children are being educated. That's wonderful! And they are getting fellowships to travel to come back home to improve local conditions!" That's the U.N.—the U.N. at the zenith of its usefulness and utility.

What was the supreme assignment of the United Nations? The supreme assignment was: "Eradicate war on this globe." Has it achieved that? No! Why? Is it because the U.N. didn't want to do it? Not at all. The U.N. should not be criticized. We are the people to criticize ourselves. We denied the U.N. the authority to achieve that objective. We organized it under the principle of diplomacy, and diplomacy is cooperation, voluntary cooperation. When diplomacy is challenged, there are only two things that an injured nation can do. It can say to the offending nation: "You shouldn't do what you are doing; it's outrageous. You are committing a travesty on the people of the territory of our country. It is a heinous crime that you are committing." Diplomacy can say: "You are performing that act. We condemn you. We protest, but help yourself. Go ahead." That's what they did in Manchuria; that's what they did in Abyssinia; but eventually, like in 1939, civilization says: "Enough, no further!" So we choose the second alternative under diplomacy. And the second alternative is - we don't say: "Help yourself and go ahead." We say then: "Enough." We do not capitulate any longer to the gangster; we don't resort to appeasement, but we fight. Only two alternatives, in the ultimate, confront diplomacy: Surrender to the gangster or fight him. If you can think of any other approach that you can use for the evaluation of diplomacy, it certainly will be welcome. But history is a confirmation of these two principles: surrender to the gangster under diplomacy, or fight him.

Now what we are interested in at this hour is just this:

to discover some formula other than war as a means of preserving peace. I don't believe that the sanity, the political sanity of the human race has been exhausted. I believe there still remains a great potential, and when a generation is summoned and they can unite their energies for the common objective, solutions then become silhouetted on the horizon, and we begin to explore them.

What is the alternative to diplomacy? There is but one that I know of, and that is the plain simple statement: "LAW." Now what is Law? Law, as Doctor Gulley taught me at Wake Forest, is a rule of action enforceable in courts. But there is not a court on earth today that can enforce an action against an individual in any world community. Diplomacy acts on collectivities, on communities, not on individuals. If we are ever to have peace, it's going to be based upon justice and the first criterion of justice is the punishment of the guilty—the individual, not his community. I violate a state law, I'm arrested; my wife and children are not. I violate a federal law, four and a half million - five million North Carolinians, they are not implicated in my act. But if we in this room tonight could project some kind of program that would jeopardize the order of the world community where diplomacy alone exists, then we would implicate the responsibility of two hundred million Americans. Collectivity!

Diplomacy has no facility for locating on the individual the responsibility of his act. And so, in bringing this thought to you, let me say the time has come in the progress of civilization to *do this one thing*: enforce order on the individual. Nothing new in it. Nobody in this generation or the previous one created such a concept. It's the teaching of history; but it's difficult to get a generation, unaccustomed to a certain procedure, to accept it. I remember in London some time, not too long ago, I telephoned to Arnold Toynbee, and I asked if he would be kind enough to extend me a short, brief conference. He did so. Knowing I'd have only a few minutes with him, I said to him: "Professor Toynbee, this generation has the knowledge, it has the experience to achieve world peace. Why is it we can't do it?" "Why," he said, "it's very simply the lack of political courage on the part of our leaders. Not a nation on earth today has a leader that is willing to jeopardize the survival of his office, for the sake of espousing a solution to world anarchy." And, as he remarked to me, he said: "You couldn't [at that time, Harold Wilson was Prime Minister]—you could not get our Harold Wilson to go before the public today, saying: 'I believe in the enforcement of order internationally on the individual.' He said, "he'd be defeated. Four years from now he probably would increase his support from thirty [he mentioned around thirty-two or three] percent to forty-four or forty-five. But eight years or twelve years from today, he'd carry the nation. But he is not prepared to risk the continuity of his political authority."

Now that is where we are punching the pith out of our problems. Our generation is making a transition from absolute nationalism to international authority—authority that can be enforced on the individual. And when you get to that point, you don't fight his nation, you arrest the guilty party. And that's the way we have organized our nation. It's the way that we have organized culture, political stability in every nation of Western Culture.

Let us, therefore, in reflection upon this thought, say: It's not to be deferred to the Greek calendar. It's now! It's you! Like the two Greek lads who went before the oracle with a bird, agreeing they would ask the oracle: "What do we have in our hands?" And the oracle will reply: "A bird." Then we will ask: "Is it dead or alive?" And if the oracle says: "It is alive," the boys, the two lads would say: "No, you're mistaken." They would crush the bird and [say] "It's dead." But if the oracle said the bird was dead, they would release the bird and it would fly away, and again they would say: "You're wrong." So they thought they had the oracle. Going in the presence of the oracle they said: "What do we have in our hands?" "A bird." "Is it dead or alive?" And the oracle replied: "*You* hold the answer in your hands."

The above transcription is a composite of two transcriptions taken from the original tape recording. The first was made by Robert's son John and myself a week or so after the speech was given. The second transcription was made some years later by Rotarian Jim Bearden after John Humber had cleared the tape of most of its background noises. I used Jim's transcription to make some corrections and fill in the blanks which John and I had been forced to leave. We are, of course, most indebted to Rotarian Ray Martinez, whose presence of mind and initiative on the evening of the address enabled us to have an original recording. Upon learning that Robert was the speaker, he rushed home, got his recording machine, and had it set up in time for the beginning of the speech.

Following the address, Robert was given a standing ovation, and Rotarians made their way to the head table to offer their congratulations. Anxious to get some notion of the effectiveness of his speech, I walked into the foyer, placed my Rotary name tag on the rack, then stood by the fireplace where I would be able to hear the comments of the Rotarians as they came in the room. Robert was among the last to enter the foyer. After placing his name tag on the rack, he turned to me and placed his arm on my shoulders as we left the building.

In accordance with our custom of long-standing, we walked to his car to enjoy another of our habitual post-Rotary discussions, this one lasting about an hour. We talked about his speech and other subjects, but one thing was foremost in Robert's thoughts at that time. He was concerned and worried that he had not been able to complete the work he wanted to do on the old Humber house. He possessed a valuable collection of approximately eight thousand volumes and he wanted to add to the house a handsome library worthy of housing that treasure.

One can only imagine the intense sorrow I felt the following afternoon, November 10, 1970, when Professor Ralph Rives telephoned me, saying that Mrs. Humber had asked him to tell me that Robert had just died of a heart attack at the Plaza Cinema where they had gone to view the film of Tolstoy's *War and Peace*.

From the parking lot in front of the cinema, I spotted a group huddled together just beyond J. C. Penney's Store, and I ran toward that group. As I approached, Lucie saw me coming and ran out to meet me. We met in the center of the parking lot east of Penney's Store, and we stood there in one another's embrace, weeping. I told Lucie in truth and sincerity that I would have been willing to go in his place; he had so much left to give to his fellowmen. I had lost a truly great friend whom I had known since my childhood; Lucie had lost the husband whom she had made the absolute center of her life. I knew that his death would shatter her life.

For months I continued to visit her, but she faded very rapidly. After suffering several strokes, she became unable to speak, and her sons, Marcel and John, placed her in a home where she was given excellent care. I visited her there and spoke to her in French and English about her family and about things in which I knew she used to be interested. It was a difficult experience for me. She kept her eyes focused on me, but I could see no clear indication that she understood what I was saying. I could only hope that she did.

Chapter XV

The people of Greenville, North Carolina, and of the state of North Carolina can be proud of their native son Robert Lee Humber. He, like all human beings on this globe, was born an individual and, like all human beings of normal birth, he was endowed with a human brain of potential greatness. He was also fortunate in having loving parents who taught him to set challenging, worthwhile goals of accomplishment for each day. Thus, early in life, he developed the strong habit of self-discipline which served him well throughout his life.

At a time when there was no government on earth with the authority to confer world citizenship upon him, Robert nevertheless considered himself a world citizen. This was due to his strong belief in the brotherhood of man and his equally strong belief in the federal democratic government of the states, a form of government which could easily be applied to nation-states.

In addition to his numerous accomplishments in behalf of the people of Greenville and of the state of North Carolina, Robert set an even higher, more difficult goal for his life-work, and he devoted many years to research at graduate and postgraduate levels in the fields of history, law, government, economics and international relations in an effort "to discover some formula other than war as a means of preserving peace."

In his search through two thousand years of history from the Peloponnesian Wars of the democratic city-states of ancient Greece to modern times, no acceptable formula appeared to him until our founding fathers rejected the Articles of Confederation in favor of a democratic federal system of government. The following excerpt taken from Robert's pamphlet on world federation written in the fall of 1940 gives a clear picture of his thought and conviction on the subject of world federation:

History has revealed but one principle by which free peoples, inhabiting extensive territories, can unite under one government without impairing their local autonomy. That principle is federation, whose virtue preserves the whole without destroying its parts and strengthens its parts without jeopardizing the whole. Federation vitalizes all nations by endowing them with security and freedom to develop their respective cultures without menace of foreign dominations. It regards as sacrosanct man's personality, his rights as an individual and as a citizen and his role as a partner with all other men in the common enterprise of building civilization for the benefit of mankind. It suppresses the crime of war by reducing to the ultimate minimum the possibility of its occurrence. It renders unnecessary the further paralyzing expenditure of wealth for belligerent activity, and cancels through the ages the mortgages of war against the fortunes and services of men. It releases the full energies, intelligence and assets of society for creative, ameliorative and redemptive work on behalf of humanity. It apprehends the entire human race as one family, human beings everywhere as brothers and all nations as component parts of an indivisible community.

There is no alternative to the federation of all nations except endless war. No substitute for The Federation of the World can organize the international community on the basis of freedom and permanent peace. Even if continental, regional or ideological federations were attempted, the governments of these federations, in an effort to make impregnable their separate defenses, would be obliged to maintain stupendously competitive armies and navies, thereby condeming humanity indefinitely to exhaustive taxation, compulsory military service and ultimate carnage, which history reveals to be not only criminally futile but positively avoidable through judicious foresight in federating all nations.

The Humber movement for world federation developed too late to exert significant influence upon the delegation of the San Francisco conference whose United Nations charter failed to grant the United Nations organization adequate power to accomplish its supreme assignment of eradicating war from this globe. Robert Lee Humber, who attended the San Francisco conference where he interviewed 80 percent of the delegates, commented on that failure saying, "It is we who should criticize ourselves for that failure. We would not grant adequate power."

Robert never turned his back on the United Nations, however. He felt that we should work with the organization and try to restructure it so it could safely be given the power it needs to carry out its assignments.

On December 7, 1954, the people of France amended the constitution of the French republic to read:

> On the morrow of the victory gained by the free peoples over the regimes which have attempted to enslave and degrade the human person, the French people proclaim anew that every human being, without distinction of race, religion, or belief, possesses inalienable and sacred rights. They solemnly reaffirm the rights and freedoms of man and citizen as enshrined in the Declaration of Rights of 1789 and the fundamental principles recognized by the laws of the Republic. In addition, they proclaim as particularly necessary in our time the following political, economic, and social principles.... On condition of reciprocity, France will accept those limitations of her sovereignty which are necessary for the organization and defense of peace.

In 1969, one year before he died, Robert wrote: "Ideas are the arsenal of progress." His ideas at that time were based on long years of intense study, reading and research at Harvard, Oxford, and the Sorbonne where he had come in contact with some of the leading minds of our time. Robert had so much more to say, but was not given the opportunity because of his sudden death on November 10, 1970.

In December of 1986, sixteen years after Robert's death, when I decided to tell this story, I first wrote a few thoughts in an effort to fix in my mind a sense of direction and purpose for this volume. I would like to repeat a few of those thoughts now as I bring this story to a close. I sincerely hope, however, that the end of this story will mark only a brief hiatus before people of North Carolina and elsewhere will seek to comprehend Robert's vision of tomorrow and carry it forward toward realization.

During the past century, man's knowledge of the physical sciences has grown by leaps and bounds. It has whisked him at incredible speed over land and sea and out into space, giving him his first thrilling glimpse from afar of the crowded little planet he calls home. During that same one hundred years, man's knowledge of world political science has become so deeply mired in the ruts of the past that it lags far behind, thus creating an awkward and dangerous gap in man's thinking.

In this computer age of atomic bombs, guided missiles, laser beams, and stockpiles of highly explosive weaponry, it may be necessary for men who still cling to the world political science reasoning of the horse-and-buggy days to grope for solutions to world political problems of today, but it is frightfully dangerous. This gap in man's knowledge must be closed without delay if an unnecessary and inexcusable world catastrophe is to be avoided.

Today, as in the past, man prays for world peace while preparing for world war. He knows that world peace *cannot* be achieved without world order, that world order *cannot* be established without world law, and that world law *cannot* be drafted and put into effect without world government. Yet, mindful of the demise of the League of Nations and frustrated by the inherent weaknesses of the United Nations, he shies away from even the thought of world government, somewhat as his grandfather's horse on the way home on a beautiful moonlit night used to shy away from a piece of white paper lying in the road. The paper, of course, was not dangerous but the shying was and *it still is.*

Both the League of Nations and the United Nations were predicated upon *treaties*, not *laws*. A law is a rule of action which can be enforced in the courts on individuals. A treaty is a voluntary agreement between collectivities. It does not have the binding force of law and cannot be enforced in the courts. "When a treaty is broken and a nation is invaded, that nation has only two alternatives: surrender or fight."* Had a world government of limited powers existed in 1930, it is quite possible that Adolph Hitler and his followers would not have been able to amass the necessary military might to carry out crushing motorized attacks on their neighbors in 1939. One of the first acts of a world government would surely be to limit the manufacture of war materiel. Millions of innocent people in Germany, as well as throughout the world, might have been spared the horrors of World War II.

"Just as the discovery of gun powder in the thirteenth century signaled the end of the Middle Ages, whose great stone fortifications were no longer adequate to protect their citizens,

---

*Quotation from Robert Lee Humber.

so the invention of the airplane and its military use in World War I signaled the end of the nation as a political entity capable of protecting its citizens."* The development of the intercontinental ballistic missile with multiple atomic warheads has since made it emphatically clear that the day of *independent, sovereign* nations has passed. Nations, like people, are *interdependent.* They are no longer individually capable of protecting the lives and property of their citizens. Without the cooperation of their neighbors, they can't even guarantee the safety of the air their citizens breathe or the purity of the water that falls on their land or that flows across their borders in rivers and streams or in subterranean aquifers.

The development of the computer and the resultant exceedingly rapid advancements now taking place in the physical sciences have thrust upon the people of this earth not only the necessity of thinking in terms of world relationships and facing critical world problems in emergency situations, but also of reacting with intelligence quickly enough to solve these problems before they explode in their faces. We measure progress today not in arithmetic but in geometric progressions. We could reach the moment of catastrophe by accident or by intent at any moment. *Yet all we need to avoid such a disaster is a little flexibility of mind.*

We have tried treaties and leagues based on treaties. *They have failed.* We have tried laws and *they have succeeded locally, statewide, and nationally.* Moreover, we have *tested* and *established* the validity of a *federal system of laws to bring people of different customs and traditions together.*

In the years that have passed since the San Francisco conference produced its charter establishing a weak United Nations, the international world, which must have binding *laws* rather than easily broken voluntary *treaties* to maintain peace and order, has become a world of lawless Chaos attracting and tempting the greed and lust for power which resides to some degree in most human beings. Men and nations have thus been subjected to a world of violence, where cruel wars of race and religion continue unabated, and faceless, frantic terrorists hijack planes and kill or capture innocent victims, whom they hold hostage while they bargain their release.

In the midst of these bloody skirmishes and endless wars into which men everywhere are being drawn, even leaders of great nations, in obvious confusion, become disconcerted. In their frustration, they forget the principles on which their na-

161

tion was built and in which their citizens still believe. They neglect their responsibilities to the United Nations and weaken it, rather than strengthen it so it can help them in their difficulties. Following the patterns of barbarism practiced by the terrorists, they commit acts of retaliation when they should know that retaliation only begets retaliation. They bend, to the breaking point, treaties which would limit the fabrication of arms. They persuade their allies to refrain from selling weapons to the fundamentalist Islamic Republic which has taken over the government of Iran and continues its blind religious orgy, murdering its own Moslem brothers in the name of Allah. Then, reversing themselves and disregarding the counsel they have given their allies, they join the merchants of death by selling their nation's weapons to those same religious extremists for profit. Still not satisfied, they use their ill-gained profit to equip rebels and mercenaries to fight other people.

This ugly, distorted picture of the "Big American Boy," which was televised in newscasts to the people of the world, dismayed his friends and allies who still remembered his concern, courage, and generosity in coming to their rescue in two world wars, both of which, we must remember, occurred as a result of bad or broken *treaties*.

In 1987 the "Big American Boy," with the Torch of World Leadership virtually in his hands, suddenly found himself watching it slip away, going back to Europe, even into the hands of a communist leader, and he muttered in his consternation, "What has happened? My government is not communist." On the contrary, it is a strong, even hawkish right wing government which referrs to the communist USSR as "an evil empire" while building up its arms production at incredible speed and expense, adding new weapons to its stockpile while rewarding unscrupulous billionaires.

But the "Big American Boy" had lost something far more valuable. He had lost, at least temporarily, his credibility; and his friends and allies with heads bowed in sadness, silently turned to examine the credentials of the new Soviet leader. They recall how proud they had been when a president of young America proposed the League of Nations and how crestfallen they became when the lovable "Big American Boy" revealed by his actions at that time that he was not yet mature enough to place the peace of all mankind above the importance he placed upon petty political jealousies within his own great nation. As he failed to ratify the League of Nations the gargantuan headlines of European newspapers expressed the depth of their disappointment: "America Abandons Her Own Beautiful Child."

In World War II the "Big American Boy" courageously reaffirmed the strength of his belief in democracy and of his loyalty to his friends and allies. At the close of that war he was again given an opportunity to lead mankind to a lasting peace. He did not turn his back on his duty, because he finally understood that a world organization representative of all mankind was necessary. He knew that no one nation could police the world and that no one nation should try to police the modern world. He also knew that this new world organization should be a democratic organization in which each nation-state would remain autonomous, each retaining its own language, customs, and traditions. But, at the San Francisco conference, he could not get a majority of his own constituency to support him in granting the United Nations the power it would need to carry out its supreme mission of maintaining peace on this globe.

In the years following the creation of that *weak* United Nations organization, its leaders knew that the excessive greed of some men and the extreme poverty and hunger of others could not exist side by side in peace indefinitely on an ever-shrinking planet. Wisely they concentrated on making great humanitarian efforts on behalf of the developing nations of the world, and they have done an excellent job. Their lack of power and inability to maintain peace, however, permitted the world to drift into a state of chaos, and eventually into a world of lawlessness, not because criminals were breaking the law, but because *there existed neither world law nor world courts with the authority to enforce world law on individuals.* We were not yet willing to establish a world-governing body even with a limited authority to write, enforce, and adjudicate *enough world law to assure peace among nations*, yet today we know that we now face global problems *which cannot be solved without coordinated global effort and action.* A few of these problems are the diminishing protective ozone shield, the global drug problem, the global nuclear proliferation problem, global terrorist actions, the global pollution problem and the dilemma of overpopulation.

Following the period during which the Reagan administration seemed incapable of communicating in a clear voice and apparently lost its credibility, general secretary Gorbachev decided to come to America to sign an arms treaty with President Reagan. The General Secretary did not come to America to bang his shoe on the table and threaten to bury us, as did a predecessor of his some years ago. Neither did he attempt to bury us alive in pompous, belligerent bombast about the superiority of communism. On the contrary, he told us quite frankly that communism in his country is not functioning as it should, and he expressed a sincere desire to end the costly arms race with the United States. He even revealed that some energizing capitalism is now permitted in small businesses in the USSR, and he announced his *perestroika* (restructuring) and *glasnost* (openess) policies.

What more could the general secretary have said without jeopardizing his position at the Kremlin? He wanted a treaty, not because he thought it would assure a lasting peace in time of crisis. Treaties never have. To the European, who has witnessed and suffered the ill effects of broken treaties, treaties are like brilliantly colored autumn leaves which charm and warm us with their beautiful but perfidious smile while making us forget the cold reality of the bone-chilling wintry winds just around the corner. He wanted the best he thought he could get under the existing circumstances, and that had to be limited to a treaty because America was still living in the past century, still thinking in terms of weak, easily broken treaties. Would Gorbachev have preferred a more permanent peace, one backed by a world organization, a world government? Yes, he would have. That fact is corroborated by the following excerpt taken from the newsletter of the United Nations Association of the United States of America, which I received by mail in January of 1988: "The United States has helped to promote important budgetary and administrative reforms at the United Nations, but even as it has done so it has steadily withdrawn its support for United Nations activities. Today the Soviet Union is seeking to fill the leadership vacuum created by this reduced United States role, and it is proposing its own ambitious agenda for strengthening the world body particularly in the area of peacekeeping."

The above newsletter excerpt certainly seems to indicate that this may, indeed, be an opportune time to invoke article 109 of the United Nations Charter and start restructuring the United Nations organization so as to give it the additional power needed to establish a system of world law.

Rather than seek to blame the right wing Reagan administration for the shortsightedness of its United Nations policy, perhaps we should look more closely at the "Big American Boy," which includes all of us. He is the key to the future of America, because a democracy can progress no faster and no further than the level of education, intelligence, and maturity of its citizenry will permit. If his schools, colleges, and universities give him a broad, basic world education on which he can continue to build throughout his life, we can have confidence that he and his nation will play an important role in the establishment of world peace through world law.

In his letter of January 19, 1922, to my mother, Robert wrote, "To be a North Carolinian and a Southerner makes me very grateful indeed to the place of my nativity."

By his life and his works, Robert Humber honored Greenville, North Carolina, his birthplace, and his native state of North Carolina, whose General Assembly of 1941 became, as a result of his efforts, the first legislative body on earth to request officially that world federation be politically ordained. Fifteen other American states followed North Carolina in making that same request, but the San Francisco conference would not grant the United Nations the authority it needed to carry out its supreme mission of eradicating war from this globe.

More than two genrations have elapsed since the UN charter was written, and we have had ample time to observe the United Nations in action. We have witnessed its strengths and its weaknesses. We are proud of its accomplishments in behalf of the developing nations, but the world has been made painfully aware that its charter fails to grant the power it must have.

Is it not time to correct that weakness? The city-states of ancient Greece developed the concept of democracy and they thrived, became enterprising and beautiful, but the richer they became, the more difficult their leaders found it to share and cooperate with the leaders of other city states. Finally during more than a generation of war they succeeded in destroying one another. Had they conceived the idea of federation they could have lived in peace with one another. Our American forefathers developed the concept of federation under whose guidance and protection the United States has become the richest and most powerful democracy. Will we now have the wisdom to share our concept of federation with the other nations of this earth in order to save and protect man's habitat and bring order to his world community? Our friends and neighbors throughout the world are anxiously watching the Big American Boy, hoping and praying that he has reached the age of reason and will act wisely. That will depend, of course, upon you and me. The concept of world federation remains the best guide we can use in restructuring the United Nations organization.

My wife and I, both retired octogenarian university professors, made gifts to East Carolina University in December of 1986 and again in 1987, in memory of Robert Lee Humber, for the purpose of advancing the concept of world federation. We are aware that our gifts are merely drops in a bucket, but we believe that it is appropriate that the filling of such buckets should begin in Greenville, North Carolina, at East Carolina University, a young, vigorous university located just four blocks from the home and birthplace of Robert Lee Humber. May our friends and neighbors throughout the world join us in this endeavor.

Appendix I: The Humber House

The Humber House, pictured in the Louis Orr pencil drawing above, stands at the corner of Washington and Fifth streets in Greenville, North Carolina. It was built by Mr. Robert Lee Humber, Sr. in the latter part of 1894 and January of 1895 at the time of his marriage. About ten years later he made an addition to the house to meet the needs of his growing family.

Within a few years after Robert Lee Humber, Jr. returned home from France in 1940 a major remodeling throughout the house began and it continued until his death in 1970. Robert Lee Humber, Jr. was a self-disciplined Christian gentleman, but he was also a renaissance man of modern times. He placed no limits on the potential of the talent with which man is endowed. The words "it cannot be done" were not a part of his vocabulary. In his travels in Europe and around the world he had seen many elegant and beautiful designs, some of which he wanted to make a part of the environment in which he and his family lived. This would require special craftsmen who were not always available. Some things would have to be purchased abroad, such as the white marble mantle for his drawing room and another for his sitting room, both of which he found in Italy. He also wanted to panel his drawing room, but he found only one man who was willing to try to find the quantity of quality walnut wood required and then only if Robert would agree to wait for delivery without pressing him. Seven years later Robert received a telephone call from South Carolina asking if he still wanted the walnut paneling. He did. Many delays occurred and occasionally building material had to stand on the lot unused for a long period of time. Due to delays over which he had no control Robert was unable to finish remodeling the Humber House before his death.

The following excerpts are taken from the writings of Robert's son, John Leslie Humber. The first, only a part of which is quoted, deals with Robert's concern for ". . . the library he so much wanted to construct at the rear of the house which would accommodate the seven or eight thousand volumes in his collection." Even in 1970, the weekend before he died, he walked over the house with his son John, drawing the plans he envisioned for that addition on the top of a cardboard box. The library would have been two stories high over the kitchen, utility room and sunroom with an entrance from the second floor back hall window as well as from a divided staircase descending from the third floor study. A balcony would have encircled the new library at the third floor level and another staircase would have given access from the library to the first floor at the rear of the house into the sunroom. Behind the utility room would have been created a greenhouse for Lucie Humber's many house plants.

"The Humber family made a gift of their home place in memory of Robert Lee Humber and Lucie Berthier Humber, to the people of Greenville and Pitt County for the nurture of their cultural heritage.

"As the result of hard work and quick action of William W. Speight and a number of community-spirited leaders, the city of Greenville was selected as the site for the North Carolina Division of Archives and History's eastern regional office. While plans were moving toward opening this facility, an application was made in 1981 to place the house on the National Register of Historic Places. The application was approved in 1983. The eastern regional office opened it doors to serve eastern North Carolina on October 1, 1983, and a public dedication was held on October 23 of that year. It is anticipated that the Robert Lee Humber House will serve the people of Greenville, Pitt County, and eastern North Carolina for many years to come."

168

Appendix II: The Fleming House

The James L. Fleming homesite at the corner of Third and Greene streets in Greenville, North Carolina (including an adjoining lot west of the present home) was purchased on January 1, 1900, in the name of Loula Victoria Fleming as a wedding present from her father, Captain Charles Alexander White.

Construction of the Fleming home was begun early in 1901 and completed in the summer of 1902. The architects, well-known in the South at that time, were Barber and Klutz of Knoxville, Tennessee. The supervising builder was Mr. C. B. West of Greenville, North Carolina. The contract between Mr. Fleming and Mr. West reveals great confidence on the part of Mr. Fleming in the ability of Mr. West but reserves to Mr. Fleming the unusual right of final decision in nearly all matters, including the right to employ and direct labor at his pleasure or to discharge anyone who, in his judgment, was incompetent.

The house, with its ornamental slate roof, handsomely structured corner turret, and long front porch (with more than one hundred linear feet of well-proportioned wrought iron grillwork), is an excellent example of a distinctive Queen Ann style of Southern architecture at the turn of the century. The

169

double front doors, with a heavy two-key mortise lock and beveled glass panels, are framed by five colorful stained glass panels across the top and upper sides of the doors. In the large rooms, which have twelve- foot ceilings, there are eight open fireplaces with no two mantles alike. Three sets of hidden double sliding doors permit the transformation of the living room, the front hall foyer, the parlor, and the dining room into one large open area. There is a large playroom on the third floor which was built for Margaret and John Winstead's children who were reared in the Fleming house.

Through foresight, the house was wired for electricity when it was built several years before Greenville had electricity. In addition to the doorbell, service buttons were installed in the floor of the dining room, beside the mantle in the living room and a wire was run through the floor in mothers bedroom to a service button on the side of her bed.

Ice was delivered in fifty to one hundred pound blocks to the back porch, where it was placed through a heavily insulated wall door approximately four and a half feet off the floor into a built-in "ice box," whose insulated compartments opened on the opposite side into the butler's pantry between the kitchen and the dining room. The iron pump on the back porch alleviated the problem of fetching water in bad weather. About twenty feet from the south side of the house was a cistern which was converted into a lily pool when city water became available.

The carriage house was originally adequate to house a surrey, a buggy, two horses, a pony, a hayloft, and a coal bin. In front of the carriage house was a small brick court where the horses were unhitched before the vehicle was rolled into the carriage house. There are in the yard today two heavy stone slabs (six feet long, one foot wide and eight inches thick) which were originally used as steps for descending from carriages. One step was located at the curb on Greene Street near an iron hitching post at the front gate, and the other was located at the side gate on Third Street near a similar hitching post. In more recent years, when Greene Street was widened, the hitching posts were removed. I have one which will eventually be returned to the property and my nephew, Dr. John L. Winstead, Jr., has the other. The wrought iron fence bordering the property on the Greene Street and Third Street sides harmonizes very well with the iron grillwork around the front porch of the house. Walks leading to the house were originally made of brick.

The real story of the Fleming house is about its originator, the man who lived and worked there and his family. James L. Fleming, a Greenville attorney, married Loula Victoria White on June 21, 1899, in the Memorial Baptist Church on Greene Street, adjoining the property which was to become the site of their future home.

Following their honeymoon to the North Carolina mountains and back to Greenville by way of Morehead City and the North Carolina seashore, they made their home in the Hotel Macon on Cotanche Street near the present location of The Daily Reflector building. They remained there until the summer of 1902, when they moved with their infant daughter, Louise, to their new home at the corner of Third of Greene streets. My sister Margaret and I were born in the home on Greene Street.

Since my father died when I was only four years old, I have little recollection of him. According to the stories I have heard since childhood, Mr. Fleming was very active in the political life of Greenville and Pitt County, serving in numerous positions with both city and county governments. He took a strong stand in behalf of those issues which he considered more important to the well-being of the people and the community. He worked diligently, for example, for the establishment of city electricity and waterworks, even after the first bond issue in 1903 had been defeated. His schooling at the Greenville Academy under the tutelage of Professor W. H. Ragsdale had whetted his appetite for knowledge. His years at Wake Forest College had broadened that knowledge and strengthened his commitment to education. His teaching experience between graduation from Wake Forest College and the study of law at the University of North Carolina transformed that commitment into an ardent desire to raise the level of instruction and quality of education in the public schools of North Carolina.

In 1904 Mr. Fleming was elected to represent the sixth senatorial district in the North Carolina Senate. In 1906 he was re-elected to the senate.

In 1907 Senator Fleming introduced a bill to establish a state normal school in eastern North Carolina. He intentionally avoided naming a specific location for the school in order to get broader support for his bill. He had seen a similar bill defeated in the 1905 session because it named Elizabeth City as the location for the school. In his bill he left the choice of location of the school open to competition among eastern communities.

In spite of the skepticism of former governor T. J. Jarvis, whom Senator Fleming had come to know quite well during the years immediately following his marriage, when both their families were living at the Hotel Macon, (Jarvis referred to his efforts in Raleigh in half of a state normal school for the east as "the folly of youth") and in spite of the strong opposite to his bill, especially from the Greensboro area, whose representatives feared competition for state funds for the Greensboro Normal School, Senator Fleming was able to garner enthusiastic support from his eastern colleagues and significant support from his western colleagues in the senate.

Before that enthusiasm could be crystallized into a solid block of support, however, rumors circulated in Raleigh that former governor T. J. Jarvis, the elder statesman of North Carolina (who still wielded considerable political influence across the state), was opposed to the bill.

Senator Fleming knew that the rumors had to be killed if his bill was to survive, and he reasoned that only Jarvis himself could effectively stop the rumors of his own opposition. He therefore devised a plan to bring the former governor to Raleigh and place him in the middle of the action, where he would be able to feel the surge of support for the bill and sense the thrill of potential success. Senator Fleming was aware that his plan contained an element of political risk to him, but this was perhaps his finest hour. He placed the passage of the bill ahead of everything and sent an urgent message to Mr. David Jordan Whichard asking him to gather the boys, come to Raleigh, and "bring the governor with you."

They did even better. They made the passage of the bill a community project. The Chamber of Commerce became involved. The Greenville Aldermen, in an adjourned meeting, made an appropriation "not exceeding $250.00 to help defray the expenses of a committee to get to Raleigh in the interest of the measure." Professor Ragsdale was made chairman of a committee of eighty Pitt County citizens, many of whom journeyed to Raleigh in support of the bill. When they arrived in Raleigh, several members of the delegation went directly to the Yarborough Hotel, where they took the precaution of protecting the former governor from his old cronies in order to prevent him from being "wooed back to the opposition"

172

before Senator Fleming arrived to take him to the Capitol.

Jarvis's appearance before the Joint Legislative Committee in the Capitol, so amply supported by outstanding citizens of Greenville and Pitt County, was a welcomed sight to his old friends in Raleigh. He was warmly received, and when he spoke convincingly in behalf of additional support for Greensboro Normal and then in favor of a state school for the east, rumors of his opposition to Senator Fleming's bill were quickly dispelled. When he left Raleigh following his second appearance before the Joint Legislative Committee, most legislators felt that the bill had a good chance of being passed during that session of the legislature. A large crowd met Jarvis at the train station when he returned to Greenville. Professor H. B. Smith presented him to the gathering as "the man who saved the day in Raleigh."

The bill was passed on March 8, 1907, as part of an "act to stimulate high school instruction in the public schools of the state and teacher training."

Following the passage of the bill Senator Fleming wasted no time in returning to Greenville and to his home at the corner of Third and Greene streets where, probably in his study, which opens directly onto the front porch near the steps on the south side of the house, he planned his strategy to win the newly authorized state school for Greenville and Pitt County. Almost daily for several weeks a horse and buggy were hitched up in the little brick court in front of the carriage house to take Fleming and Professor Ragsdale into the countryside to seek support for the school bond election. If the drive was going to be long, a small basket of fruit and sandwiches would be placed in the buggy trunk. When Mr. Fleming could not go along, his horse and buggy were used by Professor Ragsdale, who went out alone or with a friend chosen because he knew the people in the area to be visited. Meanwhile that community spirit which had figuratively taken the former governor to Raleigh on its shoulders had been kept alive. More than thirty citizens of Greenville and Pitt County were given speaking assignments in all sections of Pitt County. Mr. Fleming was given five, and he added several more impromptu speeches along the way.

According to a Daily Reflector article of April 22, 1907, "It had been previously announced that a speaking on the matter of the Eastern Training School would take place in the Court House at noon today. Judge Neal not arriving until the noon train, there was no court during the morning, and it was decided that it would be better for the speaking to take place before court."

"The ringing of the bell a little past ten o'clock assembled a good crowd in the court room."

Senator J. L. Fleming and then former governor Jarvis addressed this crowd.

The people of Greenville and Pitt County worked together in behalf of the bond elections, and their newspaper, The Daily Reflector, didn't allow a day to pass until May 14, the voting date for the county election, without the publication of an article, an editorial, or a letter in favor of the bond election. For example, on Wednesday, April 10, 1907, a brief Daily Reflector editorial stated: "What it will cost to get Eastern Training School located in Pitt County will only have to be paid once, while the benefits the county will reap from it will go on through the years without number."

Both the Greenville and Pitt County bond elections were passed and East Carolina Teachers Training School, today East Carolina University, was awarded to Greenville.

The seed for a brilliant future for Greenville and Pitt County had been sown, and James L. Fleming—and in a very real sense the house he built at the corner of Third and Greene streets—became inextricably a part of the past, present, and future of Greenville and Pitt County. Today the Fleming house is occupied by the Pitt-Greenville Chamber of Commerce which had it restored and placed in the National Register of Historic Places.